KU-319-714

PEACE + LOVE + LOW CARB

THE COOKBOOK

3 Ingredients to a healthier you!

By **Kyndra Holley**

WEBSITE

www.peaceloveandlowcarb.com

FACEBOOK

www.facebook.com/peaceloveandlowcarb

TWITTER

www.twitter.com/peacelovelocarb

PINTEREST

www.pinterest.com/kdholley3020/

--

Nutritional values contained within are estimates and guidelines only. I added them in here to help you along on your journey. Remember that ingredients can vary greatly by brand. Please read your labels and keep yourself informed of what you are putting into your body.

Also, please note that "Peace and Love" is not an actual spice. It is my belief that every dish tastes better when prepared with a little peace and love.

--

Copyright © 2013 by Kyndra Holley

All rights reserved. No part of this publication may be reproduced, distributed, or transmitted in any form or by any means, including photocopying, recording, or other electronic or mechanical methods, without the prior written permission of the publisher, except in the case of brief quotations embodied in critical reviews and certain other noncommercial uses permitted by copyright law. For permission requests, write to the publisher, addressed "Attention: Permissions Coordinator," at peacelovelowcarb@gmail.com.

ISBN-13 978-0-9891228-0-1
ISBN-10 0989122808

Published by Peace, Love, & Low Carb | Recipes by Kyndra D. Holley | Photography by Kyndra D. Holley
Book design by Milton C. Cantellay III | Printed in the United States of America

FIRST EDITION

--

Graphic design and layout by some dude with glasses.

www.miltoncantellay.com

CONTENTS

PEACE LOVE FAMILY

DEDICATION

TO BACON, for being the delicious, salty, cured meat that you are. Without you, my world would be a dark place. You make everything better. I could spend all day, every day with you and never get tired of you. The best part of waking up is bacon in my cup.

TO JACK LITTLE, for being the cutest little pup on the planet. Your snuggles have gotten me through many dark days. I've learned more about love from you than most humans could ever teach me. Thank you for always cleaning up the kitchen floor for me after I cook.

TO MY HUSBAND JON, for a million different reasons that could fill their own book. Mostly, thank you for your love, constant support and for being the best thing I've ever done with my life. I am honored to be your wife. AAA3020

TO MY MOTHER LORRINE, for the depth of love that only a mother can give and for telling me over and over throughout my whole life that I can do anything I set my mind to. It turns out you were right.

TO MY SISTER PAMELA, for being the most kind-hearted, strongest woman I know. You are my rock. It has been incredible growing up with you. What is even more incredible is the growth we are making together as adults. You'll always be my #1.

TO CRYSTAL FAZIO, for always being an amazingly, supportive friend and because no matter what, you always just seem to "get it". We are so MFEO.

TO ERIN FINNEY, for showing me that true friendships can survive through life's most profound changes, and for always supporting me while I figured out what I wanted to be when I grow up. If I told you tomorrow that I wanted to be an astronaut, you'd suit up and fly to the moon with me. I like your type.

TO MILTON CANTELLAY, for your artistic ability, graphic design skills, and the time you took to take my vision and bring it to life. None of this would have been possible without you.

SPECIAL THANKS

I would like to take a moment to give special thanks to all of the generous contributors who helped bring my vision to life. I feel as though this is my own Sally Field, Oscar moment. Without all of you, none of this would have been possible. Thank you for believing in me. There were also several anonymous donors, and although I do not know who you are, just know that you are appreciated.

INTRODUCTION

Peace, love, and low carb – 3 ingredients that brought about powerful changes in my life. It was hard to be at peace and to love myself when I was so overweight and unhealthy that I could barely stand the person staring back at me in the mirror. This isn't my first rodeo when it comes to diet and exercise. In the past, I lost 50 pounds through a low carb way of eating. I maintained for about a year and then gained it all back plus some. The way I went about it was disgusting. I pretty much survived off bunless bacon cheeseburgers and salads topped with so much ranch dressing that there was no lettuce to be seen for miles. Despite this, the weight came off pretty effortlessly, and I never even exercised. This experience gave me a false sense of what living a healthy lifestyle actually meant. I equated health with weight, and felt I was being healthy simply because I was losing weight. I felt as though I had won the lottery because the pounds were just falling off. Mind you, I still had age on my side at this point. Throughout all the years I spent being unhappy and overweight, I tried every fad diet out there. I was always looking for a quick fix. I was enamored by celebrity fad diets, infomercials, magic pills, lotions, and potions. I was willing to try everything except for good, old-fashioned, hard work. Then one day, almost out of nowhere, I just woke up. I started to see food differently. I realized what I had already known all along. I didn't put all this weight on overnight and I certainly wasn't going to lose it all overnight either. It was going to take a lot of hard work, determination and willpower to make it happen and I finally felt ready.

I'd been working in restaurants for more years than I like to account for. I love food. I love eating food. I love photographing food. I even love just being around food. You would probably hate grocery shopping with me. I did not, however, like serving food to the general public. Hungry strangers can be mean. There is no peace and love when it comes to "Hangry" people. Even though I never worked in the kitchen in any of the restaurants I worked in, I spent a lot of time there because I loved watching the whole process unfold. By working in a handful of fine dining establishments, I was exposed to ingredients and cooking techniques that I never knew existed. I grew up in a very "meat and potatoes, salt and pepper" home. Not only was I exposed to all of these new ingredients, but I was also tasting them for the first time. It was love at first bite. My palate grew to be more sophisticated over time. I was able to go out for a nice meal, analyze the flavor profiles and identify the ingredients. I began cooking at home a lot more. Each time I created something new, and it was a hit, it just fueled my passion until I felt fully ignited. This is where my passion was truly born. Food was no longer a torture device. It was no longer this thing that weighed so heavily on me. Literally and figuratively. I decided right then and there that I was going to change my life once and for all and that it wasn't going to come at the sacrifice of foods that I loved. I set out on a mission to recreate all my favorite carb-laden, comfort foods into low carb versions. I started with mac and cheese, pizza, chips... and it just spread like wildfire from there. I started taking pictures of

INTRODUCTION

CONTINUED

these cooking adventures and thus the birth of my blog in July 2011. From there I started gaining followers, while losing pounds and inches. I knew then that I was on to something.

Cooking became my catharsis; something that freed me from the negativity I felt a majority of the time. The kitchen transformed into my happy place. No need to sit on a couch in a therapist's office when I have my kitchen. My kitchen is my canvas and fresh ingredients are my muse. I love every step of recipe production, from grocery shopping, prep work, cooking, staging, photography, to clean-up. (No, I won't come clean your kitchen.) But if you ask nicely and bring me some bacon, I may just cook you dinner.

I can't explain the feeling of dreaming up a new recipe in my head, bringing it to life, only to find out that it is even better than I had imagined. Picture me standing with a giant caption bubble next to my head with a bunch of fresh ingredients shaped like puzzle pieces swirling around in it. Now picture another caption bubble full of bacon. Now see my eyes dart from side to side like a dog being teased with a treat. That pretty much sums up my thought process. Watching someone eat something I created is pure joy. If I were to eat bacon while watching someone eat something that I made, I just might explode.

Every day I learn something new about food and something new about my own body. This has been an ever-evolving process for me. I look at some of my earlier recipes, and I realize how much my own personal diet has changed since

I set out on this journey. I've cleaned up my diet considerably, and I see my recipes branching out into new, exciting directions. There is no right or wrong. I am not a nutritionist or a dietician. I am not now, nor will I ever, tell you what you should or should not eat. I am not the food police. I am just a girl with a passion for cooking, and an obsession with bacon. I know what works for me. Hopefully, you know what works for you. My take on food is a lot like my take on religion; if you believe in it and it makes you a better person, then by all means proceed with what works for you. Food can be a very private and personal thing. No one has any say about what you put into your body but you. That being said, I believe this book has something for just about everyone. All of my recipes are low carb. A vast majority of them are gluten free. "3 Ingredients To a Healthier You" is a mixture of low-carb, high fat, paleo, primal, dairy-free, sugar-free, and even vegetarian recipes.

A LOT OF LOVE WAS POURED INTO THIS BOOK, AND I HOPE YOU GET JUST AS MUCH LOVE OUT OF IT.

Peace and Love,

Kyndra D. Holley

LET'S GET SPICY!

There are a lot of spices that I have yet to cook with. One of my goals for my next project is to diversify my spice pantry and branch out into some new flavor profiles and different styles of cooking. I think it will be a fun adventure that just might produce some unanticipated deliciousness. But for the meantime, here is a list of my current pantry staples.

- [ ] **Almond Extract**
- [ ] **Basil**
- [ ] **Bay Leaves**
- [ ] **Beef Bouillon Granules**
- [ ] **Black Pepper**
- [ ] **Cajun Seasoning**
- [ ] **Cajun Trinity**
- [ ] **Cayenne**
- [ ] **Celery Salt**
- [ ] **Chicken Bouillon Granules**
- [ ] **Chili Powder**
- [ ] **Chinese 5 Spice**
- [ ] **Cinnamon**
- [ ] **Cream of Tartar**
- [ ] **Crushed Red Pepper Flakes**
- [ ] **Cumin**
- [ ] **Garlic Pepper**
- [ ] **Garlic Powder**
- [ ] **Garlic Salt**

- [ ] **Himalayan Pink Salt**
- [ ] **Italian Seasoning**
- [ ] **Lemon Extract**
- [ ] **Lemon Pepper Seasoning**
- [ ] **Onion Flakes**
- [ ] **Onion Powder**
- [ ] **Onion Salt**
- [ ] **Oregano**
- [ ] **Paprika**
- [ ] **Parsley**
- [ ] **Pumpkin Pie Spice**
- [ ] **Rubbed Sage**
- [ ] **Sea Salt**
- [ ] **Steak Seasoning**
- [ ] **Tarragon**
- [ ] **Thyme**
- [ ] **Vanilla Extract**
- [ ] **Taco Seasoning** (Recipe on page 98)
- [ ] **Blackened Seasoning** (Recipe on page 97)

In addition to these I always have fresh **chives** and **parsley**.

GROCERY LIST

This is what a typical grocery shopping list in my home might look like. Obviously it varies by what recipes I have in the works, but these are a lot of the staples I keep in my fridge and pantry. Depending on how many new recipes I make and how much we entertain, this could last about a week and a half to two weeks. Usually in that time there are a couple of trips to the store for extra vegetables and miscellaneous odds and ends. Some items, such as condiments, would not be purchased every trip as they last a long time. I just wanted to give you an idea of what my kitchen is stocked with, as well as give you some ideas to build your own grocery shopping list around. If money is tight, just buy bacon and everything will be A-okay.

MEAT/SEAFOOD/DELI
- ☐ Bacon
- ☐ Bacon
- ☐ Bacon
- ☐ Chicken Breast
- ☐ Ground Turkey
- ☐ Ground Beef
- ☐ Steak
- ☐ Pork Chops
- ☐ Pork Sausage
- ☐ Chicken Sausage
- ☐ Prawns

DAIRY AISLE
- ☐ Almond Milk
- ☐ Butter
- ☐ Cream
- ☐ Cream Cheese
- ☐ Eggs
- ☐ Fresh Mozzarella
- ☐ Parmesan Cheese
- ☐ Sharp Cheddar Cheese
- ☐ Sour Cream

PRODUCE
- ☐ Apples
- ☐ Avocado
- ☐ Bananas
- ☐ Bell Peppers
- ☐ Blueberries
- ☐ Broccoli
- ☐ Carrots
- ☐ Cauliflower
- ☐ Celery
- ☐ Cucumber
- ☐ Garlic
- ☐ Green Beans
- ☐ Green Onions
- ☐ Lemons
- ☐ Limes
- ☐ Mushrooms
- ☐ Onion
- ☐ Parsley
- ☐ Raspberries
- ☐ Red Onion
- ☐ Romaine
- ☐ Rutabaga
- ☐ Shallots
- ☐ Squash
- ☐ Strawberries
- ☐ Sweet Potato
- ☐ Swiss Chard
- ☐ Zucchini

BULK
- ☐ Raw Almonds
- ☐ Raw Cashews
- ☐ Raw Pepitas
- ☐ Spices

CONDIMENTS/MISC. AISLES
- ☐ Almond Butter
- ☐ Avocado Oil
- ☐ Balsamic Vinegar
- ☐ Beef Broth
- ☐ Black Olives
- ☐ Chicken Broth
- ☐ Coconut Oil
- ☐ Coffee
- ☐ Dijon Mustard
- ☐ Mayonnaise
- ☐ Olive Oil
- ☐ Roasted Red Peppers
- ☐ Salsa
- ☐ Tomato Paste
- ☐ Tomato Sauce
- ☐ Tuna

CHAPTER 1

APPETIZERS

BUFFALO "POTATO" WEDGES

PREP
20min

COOK
45min

PER SERVING

Calories: **235**

Carbs: **10 net g**

Fat: **15 g**

Protein: **2.5 g**

I have found rutabagas to be a great potato substitute. Pairing them with buffalo sauce and blue cheese just seemed like a no-brainer. The first thing you taste is the spicy flavor of the buffalo wing sauce and then you get the nice, sharp flavor of the blue cheese dressing.

INGREDIENTS (4 Servings)

- [ ] **2 Medium Rutabagas**
- [ ] **4 Tbs. Butter**
- [ ] **1/2 tsp. Salt**
- [ ] **1/2 tsp. Onion Powder**
- [ ] **1/8 tsp. Black Pepper**
- [ ] **1/2 Cup Buffalo Wing Sauce**
- [ ] **1/4 Cup Blue Cheese Dressing**
- [ ] **2 Green Onions** (Chopped)
- [ ] (2 Tbs. Peace and Love)

DIRECTIONS

1. Preheat oven to 400°.
2. Line a baking sheet with parchment paper.
3. Clean and peel rutabagas and slice into wedges.
4. Melt butter and stir in salt, onion powder, and black pepper. Coat rutabaga wedges liberally with seasoned, melted butter.
5. Line wedges in a single layer on baking sheet. Bake for 30 minutes.
6. Remove from oven, toss with buffalo wing sauce, place back in oven and bake for an additional 15 minutes.
7. Plate, and drizzle with blue cheese dressing. Garnish with chopped green onion.

SPICY TUNA AVOCADO BOATS

	PER SERVING
PREP 15min	Calories: **245**
COOK 15min	Carbs: **4.75 net g**
	Fat: **14.4 g**
	Protein: **17 g**

I love getting creative with avocados. These spicy tuna avocado boats are great served as a cold tuna salad or broiled as according to the directions.

INGREDIENTS (4 Servings)

- ☐ **2 Large Avocados** (Halved and pitted)
- ☐ **2 - 5oz. Can Tuna** (Drained)
- ☐ **1 Rib Celery** (Finely chopped)
- ☐ **2 Tbs. Shallots** (Chopped)
- ☐ **1 Tbs. Garlic** (Minced)
- ☐ **4 Tbs. Creamy Horseradish Sauce**
- ☐ **1/4 Cup Parmesan Cheese** (Grated)
- ☐ **1/4 Cup Parmesan Cheese** (Shredded)
- ☐ **Salt and Pepper** (To taste)
- ☐ (2 Tbs. Peace and Love)

DIRECTIONS

1. Preheat oven on Broil - High. Line a baking sheet with foil.
2. Scrape half of the avocado out of each shell.
3. In a large mixing bowl, combine avocado, tuna, celery, shallots, garlic, creamy horseradish and salt and pepper.
4. Fill avocado shells with tuna mixture. Pile it in nice and high. Top each avocado boat with grated Parmesan and shredded Parmesan.
5. Broil on medium rack for 15 minutes.

TIP: If you are not a fan of spicy foods, simply replace some or all of the creamy horseradish with mayonnaise or plain Greek yogurt.

CHICKEN PARMESAN MEATBALLS

PREP
15min

COOK
25min

PER SERVING

Serving:

3 Meatballs

Calories: **276**

Carbs: **3 net g**

Fat: **14.5 g**

Protein: **32.5 g**

This recipe is so simple and delicious. Just a few notes about it... Ground chicken is very soft and is hard to form into meatballs. But, once you get them rounded, they will keep their shape. Alternatively, you can also substitute ground turkey. I used pizza sauce in this recipe as opposed to marinara because it is significantly lower in carbs but produces a similar flavor. Make sure to read your labels and find a sauce that is a low-carb, reduced sugar version if available.

INGREDIENTS (4 Servings)

- ☐ **1 lb. Ground Chicken**
- ☐ **1/2 Cup Pizza Sauce** (Divided)
- ☐ **1/4 Cup Parmesan** (Grated)
- ☐ **3 Tbs. Italian Flat Leaf Parsley** (Chopped)
- ☐ **1 Tbs. Garlic** (Minced)
- ☐ **1/2 tsp. Italian Seasoning**
- ☐ **1/2 tsp. Onion Powder**
- ☐ **1/2 tsp. Garlic Salt**
- ☐ **1/4 tsp. Black Pepper**
- ☐ **3 oz. Mozzarella Cheese**
- ☐ (2 Tbs. Peace and Love)

DIRECTIONS

1. Preheat oven to 350°.

2. In a large mixing bowl, combine ground chicken, 2 Tbs. pizza sauce, Parmesan cheese, parsley, garlic, Italian seasoning, onion powder, garlic salt, and black pepper.

3. Form into 12 equal meatballs and place into an 8" x 11" glass baking dish.

4. Bake 25 minutes on middle rack of oven.

5. Remove from oven, spoon remaining pizza sauce over top of each meatball and top with mozzarella cheese.

6. Broil on top rack until cheese is melted and golden brown – About 2-3 minutes.

ARANCINI—FIVE CHEESE, BACON, CAULIFLOWER BITES

PER SERVING

1 Serving: **3 Balls**

Calories: **280**

Carbs: **5.4 net g**

Fat: **19.2 g**

Protein: **19.2 g**

Traditional Arancini are deep fried rice balls, coated with breadcrumbs. I re-created this traditional version into a delightfully sinful, low-carb version using riced cauliflower instead of rice. You can put any number of ingredients inside. I went with a couple of my favorites.... LOTS of cheese and bacon. I serve these with a low-carb marinara and ranch dressing. They both made for great dips.

INGREDIENTS (10 Servings)

- ☐ **5 Cups Cauliflower** (Riced)
- ☐ **1 lb. Bacon** (Cooked, and Crumbled)
- ☐ **8 oz. Cream Cheese** (Softened)
- ☐ **4 oz. Goat Cheese**
- ☐ **1/2 Cup Sharp Cheddar Cheese** (Shredded)
- ☐ **1/2 Cup Sharp Garlic White Cheddar Cheese**
- ☐ **1 1/2 Cup Parmesan Cheese** (Grated & Divided)
- ☐ **3 Cloves Garlic** (Minced)
- ☐ **1 tsp. Italian Seasoning** (Divided)
- ☐ **1/2 tsp. Sea Salt**
- ☐ **1/2 tsp. Black Pepper**
- ☐ **1 Cup Pork Rinds** (Finely Crushed)
- ☐ **1/2 Cup Panko**
- ☐ **1 tsp. Onion Powder**
- ☐ **1 tsp. Garlic Powder**
- ☐ **Oil**
- ☐ (2 Tbs. Peace and Love)

DIRECTIONS

1. In a large mixing bowl, combine riced cauliflower, bacon, cream cheese, goat cheese, cheddar cheese, white cheddar cheese, 1/2 cup grated Parmesan, minced garlic, 1/2 tsp. Italian seasoning, sea salt and pepper. Mix until all ingredients are well incorporated. Refrigerate 1-2 hours.

2. Combine crushed pork rinds, remaining 1 cup Parmesan cheese, Panko, remaining 1/2 tsp. Italian seasoning, onion powder and garlic powder. Pour mixture in a thin layer on a large plate.

3. Heat an inch of oil over medium-high heat. I use a non-stick wok for stove-top deep frying. The high sides reduce splatter and make clean up a cinch.

4. Remove cauliflower mixture from refrigerator and roll into 30 even balls, approximately an inch and a half to two inches in diameter.

5. Roll each ball in breading mixture until evenly and liberally coated.

6. Once oil is hot and begins to bubble, drop cauliflower balls into the oil, 5 or 6 at a time. Using tongs to turn them, fry until they are an even golden brown all over—about 3-4 minutes each side.

7. After removing cauliflower balls from oil, allow to cool on a paper towel to soak up excess grease. This will also give the breading a chance to crisp up so that it stays on.

TIP: To rice the cauliflower you can pulse it in a food processor or even just use a cheese grater. I used a cheese grater.

GRILLED PORTOBELLO CAPRESE

PREP
30min

COOK
15min

PER SERVING

Calories: **186**

Protein: **12 g**

Carbs: **8.75 net g**

Fat: **16.75 g**

The flavor combination of tomato, fresh mozzarella, and basil is a timeless classic. Add balsamic vinegar and kalamata olives, and you have a whole new level of flavor. Sometimes when I make this dish, I lightly season and grill a chicken breast, cube it, and mix it in with the rest of the ingredients and then place the whole thing on a bed of romaine. It makes an awesome grilled chicken portobello caprese salad. Delish!

INGREDIENTS (6 Servings)

- ☐ **4 Large Portobello Mushroom Caps**
- ☐ **1/4 Cup Balsamic Vinegar**
- ☐ **2 Cloves Garlic** (Minced)
- ☐ **2 Tbs. Olive Oil**
- ☐ **1/2 tsp. Sea Salt**
- ☐ **1/2 tsp. Onion Powder**
- ☐ **1/8 tsp. Black Pepper**
- ☐ **8 oz. Fresh Mozzarella Cheese**
- ☐ **2 Beefsteak Tomatoes**
- ☐ **12 Fresh Basil Leaves** (Chopped)
- ☐ **5 Kalamata Olives** (Sliced)
- ☐ (2 Tbs. Peace and Love)

DIRECTIONS

1. De-stem mushrooms and rinse thoroughly.

2. In a medium bowl, combine balsamic vinegar, garlic, olive oil, sea salt, onion powder, and pepper. This will be your marinade.

3. In a large dish with high sides, place the mushrooms in a single layer, gill side up, and pour the marinade over the mushrooms. Allow to marinate in the refrigerator for 1 hour. Keep excess marinade that seeps from mushrooms and collects in the dish.

4. Heat a lightly oiled grill pan over medium heat. Grill mushroom caps, gill side up—10 minutes.

5. Chop fresh mozzarella, tomatoes and basil and combine in a large mixing bowl. Toss in remaining marinade. Divide mixture among the grilled Portobello caps.

6. Garnish with sliced kalamata olives.

BACON, BLUE CHEESE, & CARAMELIZED ONION STUFFED MUSHROOMS

PREP
30min

COOK
1hr

PER SERVING

Calories: **245**

Protein: **10.3 g**

Carbs: **6.3 net g**

Fat: **18 g**

I know the title is a mouthful but so are these mushrooms... a mouthful of goodness. Here is a little tip for cooking these beauties. Use a mini muffin tin to hold the mushrooms upright. It will hold them snugly in place and keep them from falling over and losing their toppings.

INGREDIENTS (4 Servings)

- ☐ **1 lb. Cremini Mushrooms**
- ☐ **2 Small Onions** (Thinly Sliced)
- ☐ **3 Tbs. Butter**
- ☐ **2 Tbs. Garlic** (Minced)
- ☐ **4 Slices Thick Cut Bacon** (Cooked Crisp and Crumbled)
- ☐ **8 oz. Cream Cheese** (Softened)
- ☐ **1/2 Cup Blue Cheese Crumbles**
- ☐ **1/4 Parmesan Cheese** (Shredded)
- ☐ **Salt and Pepper** (To Taste)
- ☐ (2 Tbs. Peace and Love)

DIRECTIONS

1. Thoroughly wash mushrooms and remove stems. Finely chop the stems.

2. In a large sauté pan over low-medium heat, add onions, butter, garlic and salt and pepper. Cook until onions are nice and caramelized—about 30 minutes.

3. In a large mixing bowl, combine chopped mushroom stems, caramelized onions, bacon, softened cream cheese, and blue cheese crumbles. Mix until all ingredients are well combined.

4. Stuff each mushroom cap with mixture. Bake at 350° for 25 minutes.

5. Take mushrooms out of the oven and top each one with shredded Parmesan. Bake 10 additional minutes.

TIP: Many people either do not care for, or are allergic to blue cheese. An herbed feta or goat cheese, would make an excellent substitution.

BUFFALO CHICKEN DEVILED EGGS

PREP
20min

COOK
12min

PER SERVING

Calories: **112**

Protein: **7.5 g**

Carbs: **1.3 net g**

Fat: **8.5 g**

When this idea came to me I wasn't sure if I was about to develop some new genius creation or perhaps the oddest combination ever. The end result was incredibly delicious and just seemed to make perfect sense. I like to garnish these with some chopped green onion. It adds a nice contrasting color to the presentation.

INGREDIENTS (6 Servings)

- ☐ **6 Large Eggs**
- ☐ **6 oz. Cooked Chicken** (Chopped)
- ☐ **1/4 Cup Blue Cheese Crumbles**
- ☐ **1/4 Cup Buffalo Wing Sauce**
- ☐ **1/2 Rib Celery**
- ☐ **2 Tbs. Blue Cheese Dressing**
- ☐ **1/4 Small Sweet Onion**
- ☐ (2 Tbs. Peace and Love)

DIRECTIONS

1. Hard boil the eggs. See tip at the bottom of the page for the perfect hard-boiled eggs.

2. While eggs are boiling, chop up the chicken and celery.

3. Peel the eggs and slice in half lengthwise.

4. In a large mixing bowl, combine the egg yolks, chicken, blue cheese crumbles, buffalo wing sauce, celery, and blue cheese dressing.

5. Use a microplane grater to grate the onion over the bowl. The juice from the onion will add a lot of flavor to the mixture. Mix until all ingredients are well incorporated.

6. Put mixture into a plastic bag. Squeeze the mixture to one corner of the bag and snip off the corner. Use this to pipe the mixture into the eggs.

TIP: This is how I make perfect hard-boiled eggs. Place the eggs in a large sauce pan with cold water. Add enough water that the eggs are fully submerged. Over high heat bring water to a rolling boil. Once the water is boiling, remove the pan from the heat, cover and let sit for 12 minutes.

DEEP FRIED MUSHROOMS

PREP
30min

COOK
30min

PER SERVING

Calories: **414**

Protein: **32 g**

Carbs: **4.5 net g**

Fat: **30 g**

Missing those delicious fried appetizers at your favorite restaurant? This low carb version will curb that craving. I served them with an artichoke garlic aioli sauce. You can find that recipe on page 86. I used jarred, whole button mushrooms to make these. Normally I use fresh mushrooms in my recipes. However, with this recipe using jarred mushrooms is the way to go. The breading crisps really fast and fresh mushrooms would not have enough time to cook all the way through without burning the breading.

INGREDIENTS (4 Servings)

- ☐ **2 Jars Whole Button Mushrooms**
- ☐ **2 Cups Pork Rinds** (Crushed)
- ☐ **1 Cup Parmesan Cheese** (Grated)
- ☐ **1 Tbs. Garlic Powder**
- ☐ **1/2 Cup Heavy Cream**
- ☐ **1 Large Egg**
- ☐ **Oil**
- ☐ (2 Tbs. Peace and Love)

DIRECTIONS

1. Drain liquid from mushrooms and pat dry with a paper towel.

2. Place pork rinds, Parmesan cheese, and garlic powder into a food processor and pulse until the mixture becomes fine and flour like.

3. In a shallow dish, combine heavy cream and egg to make a wash. Fork whisk until they are well blended

4. Heat an inch of oil over medium-high heat. I use a non-stick wok for stove-top deep frying. The high sides reduce splatter and make clean up a cinch.

5. Coat each mushroom in the breading mixture, dip in the egg wash, and then coat in the breading mixture a second time.

6. Once the oil is hot and begins to bubble, drop breaded mushrooms in oil and fry until breading is crispy—about 2 minutes each side. Try not to flip the mushrooms too many times as this will cause the breading to fall off.

7. After removing mushrooms from oil, allow to cool on a paper towel to soak up excess grease. This will also give the breading a chance to crisp up so that it stays on.

FRIED MOZZARELLA BALLS

PREP 30min

COOK 30min

PER SERVING

Calories: **400**

Protein: **22 g**

Carbs: **4 net g**

Fat: **32 g**

These fried mozzarella balls are wonderful served with a low-carb, garlic marinara or ranch dressing. To make these gluten-free, simply replace the panko with additional pork rinds or parmesan.

INGREDIENTS (4 Servings)

- ☐ **1 - 12oz. Container Marinated Fresh Mozzarella Balls**
- ☐ **1 Large Egg**
- ☐ **1/4 Cup Heavy Cream**
- ☐ **1 Cup Pork Rinds** (Crushed)
- ☐ **1/4 Cup Panko**
- ☐ **1/2 Cup Parmesan Cheese** (Grated)
- ☐ **1/2 tsp. Garlic Powder**
- ☐ **1/2 tsp. Onion Powder**
- ☐ **1/2 tsp. Oregano**
- ☐ **1/2 tsp. Italian Seasoning**
- ☐ **Oil**
- ☐ (2 Tbs. Peace and Love)

DIRECTIONS

1. Heat an inch of oil over high heat. I use a non-stick wok for stove-top deep frying. The high sides reduce splatter and make clean up a cinch.

2. In a shallow bowl, combine heavy cream and egg and fork whisk.

3. Mix pork rinds, panko, Parmesan cheese, garlic powder, onion powder, oregano and Italian seasoning. Pour mixture on a large plate, in a thin layer.

4. Roll each mozzarella ball in breading mixture, dredge in the egg wash, and roll in the breading mixture a second time.

5. Once oil is hot and begins to bubble, drop breaded mozzarella balls into the oil. Using tongs, turn them continuously until they are golden brown and crisp. This will happen very fast. It is important to use a high heat to flash fry the breading without melting the cheese.

TIP: Be sure to check the smoke point for your oil to ensure that it is a suitable oil for frying. Albeit an expensive option, on the rare occasion that I fry foods, I use avocado oil. It has a smoke point of over 500° and is among the healthiest of the oils.

CHICKEN CLUB AVOCADO BOATS

PREP
20min

COOK
20min

PER SERVING

Calories: **380**

Protein: **28 g**

Carbs: **4.5 net g**

Fat: **27.5 g**

I love getting creative with avocados. I could probably write an entire cookbook based around this deliciously, creamy fruit. I think I just might do that.

INGREDIENTS (4 Servings)

- ☐ **1 lb. Boneless, Skinless Chicken Breast** (Cooked and Cubed)
- ☐ **2 Avocados** (Halved, Pitted and Cubed)
- ☐ **2 Tbs. Garlic** (Minced & Divided)
- ☐ **2 Tbs. Lime Juice**
- ☐ **5 Strips Bacon** (Cooked Crisp, and Crumbled)
- ☐ **1/4 Cup Red Onion** (Chopped)
- ☐ **8 Grape Tomatoes** (Halved)
- ☐ **4 Tbs. Mayonnaise**
- ☐ **Salt and Pepper** (To Taste)
- ☐ (2 Tbs. Peace and Love)

DIRECTIONS

1. Trim excess fat from chicken, cook and cube.

2. Halve the avocados, remove pits and scoop avocado from shells. Set shells aside as you will be using them later.

3. In a medium mixing bowl, combine three of the avocado halves, 1 Tbs. garlic, lime juice, and a dash of salt and pepper. Fork mash until ingredients are well incorporated.

4. For the chicken salad – Cut remaining avocado into chunks. In a large mixing bowl combine avocado, chicken, bacon, red onion, tomatoes, mayo, 1 Tbs. garlic, and a pinch of salt and pepper. Stir until completely mixed

5. Divide the mashed avocado mixture among the 4 avocado shells. Top each one with a heaping mound of the chicken salad.

TIP: Cook the chicken in any manner you desire. I like to cut the chicken breasts into tender sized pieces and pan-sear them in butter. It makes for a slightly crispy outside and an extremely juicy inside.

ANOTHER TIP: If you do not eat mayonnaise, you can replace it in this recipe with plain Greek yogurt.

BONELESS BUFFALO WINGS

 PREP
30min

 COOK
30min

PER SERVING

Calories: **350**

Protein: **40 g**

Carbs: **0.5 net g**

Fat: **15 g**

Before creating this recipe I never thought I would be able to mask the taste of pork rinds. Like a lot of people, I do not care for them at all. BUT, with this recipe I was able to re-create one of my favorite bar foods without ever missing traditional breading.

INGREDIENTS (4 Servings)

- ☐ **1 lb. Boneless, Skinless Chicken Breast**
- ☐ **1 1/2 Cups Pork Rinds** (Crushed)
- ☐ **1/2 Cup Parmesan Cheese** (Grated)
- ☐ **1/2 tsp. Garlic Powder**
- ☐ **3/4 Cup Buffalo Wing Sauce**
- ☐ **2 Tbs. Butter**
- ☐ **Olive Oil**
- ☐ (2 Tbs. Peace and Love)

DIRECTIONS

1. Trim excess fat off chicken breast and cut into large chunks.

2. In a food processor, combine pork rinds, Parmesan cheese, and garlic powder and pulse until ingredients are well combined and moderately fine. Pour mixture onto a plate, in a thin layer.

3. Heat an inch of olive oil over medium-high heat. I use a non-stick wok for stove-top deep frying. The high sides reduce splatter and make clean up a cinch.

4. Press the chicken chunks firmly into the breading mixture, coating both sides (Doing it this way will help the breading bind to the chicken much better than just shaking them in the breading mixture.)

5. Once olive oil is hot and begins to bubble, drop the breaded chicken into the oil. Using tongs, flip the chicken pieces a few times until they are golden brown and crisp on both sides—about 3 minutes each side.

6. After removing chicken from oil, allow to cool on a paper towel to soak up excess grease. This will also give the breading a chance to crisp up so that it stays on.

7. Melt the butter and mix with buffalo wing sauce. Lightly toss the Chicken in the sauce.

CHEDDAR JALAPENO BACON BISCUITS

PREP
30min

COOK
30min

PER SERVING

Serving: **1 Biscuit**

Calories: **154**

Protein: **4.2 g**

Carbs: **2 net g**

Fat: **9.25 g**

These biscuits are simply delicious and extremely versatile. They pair well with a hearty soup or chili. They are even amazing topped with a fried egg and served for breakfast. You can change the meat and cheeses in the recipe to make a huge variety of other savory biscuits and muffins. My low carb bake mix of choice is Tova CarbQuik Bake Mix.

INGREDIENTS (12 Servings)

- ☐ **4 oz. Cream Cheese** (Softened)
- ☐ **1 Egg**
- ☐ **1 1/2 Cups Sharp Cheddar Cheese** (Shredded)
- ☐ **6 Strips Bacon** (Cooked Crisp, and Crumbled)
- ☐ **10 Pickled Jalapeno Slices** (Diced)
- ☐ **1 Tbs. Garlic** (Minced)
- ☐ **1/4 tsp. Italian Seasoning**
- ☐ **1/4 tsp. Onion Salt**
- ☐ **1/4 tsp. Garlic Powder**
- ☐ **1 1/4 Cups Low Carb Bake Mix**
- ☐ **1/4 Cup Heavy Cream**
- ☐ **1/4 Cup Water**
- ☐ (2 Tbs. Peace and Love)

DIRECTIONS

1. Preheat oven to 350°.

2. Using a hand mixer, in a large mixing bowl, cream together cream cheese and egg until well blended and smooth.

3. Using a rubber spatula, fold cheddar cheese, bacon, jalapenos, minced garlic, Italian seasoning, onion salt, and garlic powder into mixture.

4. Add low carb bake mix, heavy cream, and water and stir until all ingredients are well incorporated.

5. Drop heaping mounds of the dough onto a buttered muffin top pan or cookie sheet. Mixture should make 12 biscuits.

6. Bake for 20 minutes. Allow to cool on a cooling rack for 30 minutes before serving.

NACHO CHIPS

PREP
15min

COOK
25min

PER SERVING

Calories: **274**

Protein: **5 g**

Carbs: **.5 net g**

Fat: **3.5 g**

I created these chips to use for nachos. When cooked correctly they simulate the crunch of a chip perfectly. Simply top them with all of your favorite nacho ingredients and you have a low carb version of an old favorite. I like to top them with seasoned ground beef, tomatoes, onion, jalapeno, olives, guacamole, sour cream and salsa.

INGREDIENTS (4 Servings)

- ☐ **2 Cups Sharp Cheddar Cheese** (Shredded)
- ☐ **1/2 Cup Parmesan Cheese** (Grated)
- ☐ **1 tsp. Cumin**
- ☐ **1 tsp. Garlic Powder**
- ☐ **1/2 tsp. Onion Powder**
- ☐ **1/2 tsp. Chili Powder**
- ☐ (2 Tbs. Peace and Love)

DIRECTIONS

1. Preheat oven to 400°.
2. Line a baking sheet with parchment paper and spray lightly with non-stick cooking spray.
3. Sprinkle cheddar cheese onto parchment paper and spread out as thin as you can.
4. Sprinkle grated Parmesan evenly on top of cheddar cheese.
5. Combine cumin, garlic powder, onion powder and chili powder and sprinkle over top of the cheeses.
6. Bake on middle rack for 8-10 minutes. Check on it every couple of minutes to avoid burning the cheese. Remove from oven and allow to cool on a cooling rack for 10 minutes.
7. Remove baked cheese from parchment paper and using either kitchen shears or a pizza cutter, cut the cheese into strips. Then cut each strip into triangles.
8. Place chips back on parchment paper and broil on high for 2 minutes. Monitor them closely so they do not burn.
9. Remove chips from oven and allow to cool and crisp up before serving—about 30 minutes.

ALMOND-PARMESAN CRUSTED CHICKEN NUGGETS

PREP 30min

COOK 25min

PER SERVING

Calories: **403**

Protein: **35 g**

Carbs: **3 net g**

Fat: **28 g**

The almond Parmesan breading in this recipe is also delightful on fish as well. This healthier version of a timeless childhood favorite is a great way to get your kids to eat healthier while still giving them the foods they love.

INGREDIENTS (4 Servings)

- ☐ **1 lb. Boneless, Skinless Chicken Breast**
- ☐ **1 Cup Blanched Almonds**
- ☐ **1/2 Cup Parmesan Cheese** (Grated)
- ☐ **1/2 tsp. Onion Powder**
- ☐ **1/2 tsp. Italian Seasoning**
- ☐ **1/4 Cup Heavy Cream**
- ☐ **1 Large Egg**
- ☐ **Pinch Cayenne Pepper**
- ☐ **Olive Oil**
- ☐ (2 Tbs. Peace and Love)

DIRECTIONS

1. Trim excess fat from chicken and cut into nugget sized pieces.

2. Heat an inch of olive oil over medium-high heat. I use a non-stick wok for stove-top deep frying. The high sides reduce splatter and make clean up a cinch.

3. Place almonds, Parmesan cheese, onion powder and Italian seasoning into a food processor and pulse until the mixture becomes fine and flour like.

4. In a shallow dish, combine heavy cream, egg, and pinch of cayenne pepper. Fork whisk until well combined.

5. Coat chicken pieces in breading mixture, dredge in heavy cream/egg wash, and then coat a second time in breading mixture.

6. Once the olive oil is heated and begins to bubble, drop chicken nuggets in oil and fry until cooked all the way through and crispy—about 3 minutes each side. Try not to flip the nuggets too many times as this will cause the breading to come off.

7. After removing chicken from oil, allow to cool on a paper towel to soak up excess grease. This will also give the breading a chance to crisp up so that it stays on.

> **TIP:** Almond flour can get quite expensive. It is simple to make your own. Simply buy blanched almonds and pulse them in a food processor until they make a fine powder. Be careful not to over pulse them as the almonds will turn into a paste.

BACON GUACAMOLE DEVILED EGGS

PREP
20min

COOK
12min

PER SERVING

Calories: **140**

Protein: **7.5 g**

Carbs : **2.7 net g**

Fat: **10.5 g**

This is the perfect game day appetizer. Bring this to a party and you are sure to impress. Not to mention that it combines two of the usual suspects at any party...deviled eggs and guacamole.

INGREDIENTS (6 Servings)

- ☐ **6 Large Eggs**
- ☐ **4 Strips Thick Cut Bacon** (Cooked Crisp and Crumbled)
- ☐ **1 Large Avocado**
- ☐ **2 Tbs. Salsa**
- ☐ **1 Tbs. Garlic** (Minced)
- ☐ **1 Tbs. Lime Juice**
- ☐ **1 Tbs. Dried Onion Flakes**
- ☐ **½ tsp. Garlic Salt**
- ☐ **Pinch Cayenne Pepper**
- ☐ (2 Tbs. Peace and Love)

DIRECTIONS

1. Hard boil the eggs. See tip at the bottom of the page for the perfect hard-boiled eggs.

2. Peel the eggs and slice in half lengthwise.

3. In a large mixing bowl, fork mash the avocado. To the bowl, add egg yolks, bacon, salsa, garlic, lime juice, onion flakes, garlic salt, and cayenne pepper. Mix until all ingredients are well incorporated.

4. Put mixture into a plastic bag. Squeeze the mixture to one corner of the bag and snip off the corner. Use this to pipe the mixture into the eggs.

TIP: This is how I make perfect hard-boiled eggs. Place the eggs in a large sauce pan with cold water. Add enough water that the eggs are fully submerged. Over high heat bring water to a rolling boil. Once the water is boiling, remove the pan from the heat, cover and let sit for 12 minutes.

CHAPTER 2

SOUPS & SALADS

LENTIL AND ITALIAN SAUSAGE SOUP

PREP
30min

COOK
6hours

PER SERVING

Serving: **1 Cup**

Calories: **195**

Carbs: **4.9 net g**

Fat: **14 g**

Protein: **11 g**

Many years ago I worked at an Italian restaurant that had lentil and Italian sausage soup on the menu. It was not something I would normally be drawn to on a menu and if it wasn't for the fact that we had to sample the entire menu, I may have never tried it. One taste and I began my love affair with this amazingly comforting winter soup. I set out to re-create that very soup and the memories tied to it. I am proud to announce that it was a huge success. If you are skeptical, give it one taste and you will become a believer.

INGREDIENTS (16 Servings)

- ☐ **1 1/2 Cups Lentils**
- ☐ **5 Cups Chicken Broth**
- ☐ **1 1/2 lb. Italian Sausage**
- ☐ **2 Tbs. Butter**
- ☐ **2 Tbs. Olive Oil**
- ☐ **1 Packed Cup Fresh Spinach Leaves**
- ☐ **1/2 Cup Carrot** (Diced)
- ☐ **1/2 Cup Onion** (Diced)
- ☐ **3 Tbs. Garlic** (Minced)
- ☐ **1 Leek** (Cleaned and Trimmed)
- ☐ **1 Rib Celery** (Diced)
- ☐ **1 Cup Heavy Cream**
- ☐ **1/2 Cup Parmesan Cheese** (Grated)
- ☐ **2 Tbs. Dijon Mustard**
- ☐ **2 Tbs. Red Wine Vinegar**
- ☐ **Salt and Pepper** (To Taste)
- ☐ (2 Tbs. Peace and Love)

DIRECTIONS

1. Heat slow cooker on low setting.
2. Thoroughly rinse lentils, and add to slow cooker with chicken broth.
3. In a large skillet over medium-high heat, brown sausage in olive oil and butter. Using a slotted spoon, remove sausage from pan, reserving liquid. Add sausage to slow cooker.
4. Add spinach, carrots, onions, garlic, leek, celery and a little salt and pepper to liquid in pan. Sauté vegetables over medium heat until tender—about 10 minutes. Add vegetables to slow cooker.
5. Add heavy cream, Parmesan cheese, Dijon mustard and red wine vinegar to slow cooker. Stir until mixed.
6. Cover and cook on low 6-8 hours.

CHICKEN BACON CHOWDER

PREP
45min

COOK
6hours

PER SERVING
Serving: **1 cup**
Calories: **236**
Carbs:
2.5 net grams
Fat: **13 g**
Protein: **16 g**

This chowder is deliciously rich and flavorful. If you are looking to impress your friends with your cooking skills, this would be the dish to make them. Although it keeps well in the fridge, good luck having any leftovers.

INGREDIENTS (16 Servings)

- ☐ **4 Cloves Garlic** (Minced)
- ☐ **1 Shallot** (Finely Chopped)
- ☐ **1 Leek** (Cleaned, Trimmed, and Sliced)
- ☐ **2 Ribs Celery** (Diced)
- ☐ **6 oz. Cremini Mushrooms** (Sliced)
- ☐ **1 Medium Sweet Onion** (Thinly Sliced)
- ☐ **4 Tbs. Butter** (Divided)
- ☐ **2 Cups Chicken Broth** (Divided)
- ☐ **1 lb. Boneless, Skinless Chicken Breasts**
- ☐ **8 oz. Cream Cheese**
- ☐ **1 Cup Heavy Cream**
- ☐ **1 lb. Bacon** (Cooked Crisp, and Crumbled)
- ☐ **1 tsp. Salt**
- ☐ **1 tsp. Black Pepper**
- ☐ **1 tsp. Garlic Powder**
- ☐ **1 tsp. Thyme**
- ☐ (2 Tbs. Peace and Love)

DIRECTIONS

1. Heat slow cooker on low setting.

2. To slow cooker, add garlic, shallot, leek, celery, mushrooms, onion, 2 Tbs. butter, 1 cup chicken broth, and salt and pepper. Cover, and cook vegetables on low for 1 hour.

3. Complete this next step while the vegetables are cooking; in a large skillet over medium-high heat, pan-sear the chicken breasts in the remaining 2 Tbs. butter until they are browned on both sides—about 5 minutes each side. (Chicken will not be fully cooked during this stage.)

4. Remove chicken from pan and set aside. De-glaze the pan with the remaining 1 cup of chicken broth. Using a rubber spatula, scrape up any bits of chicken that may be stuck to the pan. Add chicken stock to slow cooker.

5. Add heavy cream, cream cheese, garlic powder, and thyme to slow cooker. Stir until well combined and there are no longer any visible chunks of cream cheese.

6. Once chicken has cooled, cut into cubes and add to slow cooker, along with bacon. Stir until all ingredients are well combined. Cover and let cook for 6-8 hours.

BROCCOLI CHEDDAR SOUP

PREP
30min

COOK
7hours

PER SERVING

Serving: **1 Cup**

Calories: **235**

Carbs: **5 net g**

Fat: **18 g**

Protein: **13 g**

This thick, cheesy soup is not for the faint of heart. But if you are a complete quesophile like myself, then you have come to the right place. This soup freezes and reheats very well. I recommend reheating it on the stove top and adding a touch of cream.

INGREDIENTS (20 Servings)

- ☐ **1 Medium Onion** (Chopped)
- ☐ **5 Cloves Garlic** (Minced)
- ☐ **2 Tbs. Butter**
- ☐ **1 Medium Head Cauliflower** (Cut Into Florets)
- ☐ **1 1/2 lbs. Broccoli** (Cut Into Florets)
- ☐ **2 Leeks** (Cleaned, Trimmed, and Sliced)
- ☐ **32 oz. Chicken Broth**
- ☐ **2 Cups Heavy Cream**
- ☐ **4 Cups Sharp Cheddar Cheese** (Shredded)
- ☐ **2 Cups Parmesan Cheese** (Grated)
- ☐ **Salt and Pepper** (To Taste)
- ☐ (2 Tbs. Peace and Love)

DIRECTIONS

1. Heat slow cooker on high setting.

2. In a large sauté pan, over low-medium heat, add onion, garlic, butter and salt and pepper. Sauté onions until they are caramelized—about 30 minutes.

3. To slow cooker, add caramelized onions, cauliflower, broccoli, leeks, chicken broth, heavy cream and a pinch of salt and pepper. Mix all ingredients together. Cover and cook on high for 5-6 hours.

4. After 5-6 hours the vegetables should be nice and tender. Using a potato masher, mash up the vegetables. You can use an immersion blender for this also, but the vegetables should be soft enough that you can just give them a quick mash and have a nice, thick textured soup.

5. Add cheddar and Parmesan cheese, more salt and pepper (if desired) and cook on high for 1 additional hour.

CLAM CHOWDER

PREP
15min

COOK
6hours

x6

PER SERVING

Calories: **276**

Carbs: **3.75 net g**

Fat: **28.5 g**

Protein: **12 g**

This is a nice, hearty New England style chowder. The only thing missing are the potatoes. If you were looking to add something to simulate the potato in a typical clam chowder, simply add some diced rutabaga or cauliflower to the recipe.

INGREDIENTS (12 Servings)

- ☐ **1/4 Cup Chicken Broth**
- ☐ **4 Cloves Garlic** (Minced)
- ☐ **1 Shallot** (Thinly Sliced)
- ☐ **1 Leek** (Cleaned, Trimmed, & Sliced)
- ☐ **2 Ribs Celery** (Diced)
- ☐ **1 Medium Onion** (Chopped)
- ☐ **2 Tbs. Butter**
- ☐ **2 tsp. Sea Salt**
- ☐ **1 tsp. Black Pepper**
- ☐ **3 - 10 oz. Cans Fancy Whole Baby Clams** (Drained)
- ☐ **2 Cups Clam Juice**
- ☐ **1 lb. Thick Cut Bacon** (Cooked Crisp, & Crumbled)
- ☐ **8 oz. Cream Cheese** (Softened)
- ☐ **1 1/2 Cups Heavy Cream**
- ☐ **1 tsp. Garlic Powder**
- ☐ **1 tsp. Thyme**
- ☐ (2 Tbs. Peace and Love)

DIRECTIONS

1. Heat slow cooker on low setting.

2. To slow cooker, add chicken broth, garlic, shallot, leek, celery, onion, butter, and salt and pepper. Cover, and cook vegetables on low for 1 hour.

3. To the slow cooker, add clams, clam juice and bacon.

4. Add cream cheese, heavy cream, garlic powder and thyme. Continue mixing until there are no visible clumps of cream cheese and all ingredients are well incorporated.

5. Cover and cook for 6-8 hours.

KICKIN' CHILI

PREP
30min

COOK
6hours

PER SERVING

Serving: **1 Cup**

Calories: **137**

Carbs:

4.7 net grams

Fat: **5 g**

Protein: **16 g**

This recipe was my maiden voyage with my new slow cooker. It was also the first time I ever made chili. It turned out to be spectacularly, spicy success. This recipe is so good, you won't even miss the beans. This chili does have a little bit of kick to it. If you do not like spicy, you can always omit the cayenne and/or the jalapenos.

INGREDIENTS (16 Servings)

- ☐ **2 1/2 lbs. Lean Ground Beef**
- ☐ **1 Medium Red Onion** (Chopped and Divided)
- ☐ **4 Tbs. Garlic** (Minced)
- ☐ **3 Large Ribs Celery** (Diced)
- ☐ **1/4 Cup Pickled Jalapeno Slices**
- ☐ **1 – 6 oz. Can Tomato Paste**
- ☐ **1 – 14.5 oz. Can Tomatoes & Green Chilies**
- ☐ **1 - 14.5 oz. Can Stewed Tomatoes with Mexican Seasoning**
- ☐ **2 Tbs. Worcestershire Sauce**
- ☐ **4 Tbs. Chili Powder**
- ☐ **2 1/2 Tbs. Cumin** (Mounded)
- ☐ **2 tsp. Salt**
- ☐ **1 tsp. Garlic Powder**
- ☐ **1 tsp. Onion Powder**
- ☐ **1 tsp. Oregano**
- ☐ **1 tsp. Black Pepper**
- ☐ **1/2 tsp. Cayenne**
- ☐ **1 Bay Leaf**
- ☐ (2 Tbs. Peace and Love)

DIRECTIONS

1. Heat slow cooker on low setting.

2. In a large skillet over medium-high heat, add ground beef, half of the onion, 2 Tbs. minced garlic, and a pinch of salt and pepper. Once the beef is browned, drain excess grease from pan.

3. Transfer ground beef mixture to slow cooker. Add remaining onions and garlic, celery, jalapenos, tomato paste, tomatoes and chilies (with liquid), stewed tomatoes (with liquid), Worcestershire sauce, chili powder, cumin, salt, cayenne, garlic powder, onion powder, oregano, black pepper, and bay leaf.

4. Stir until all ingredients are well combined. Cook on low 6-8 hours.

CHICKEN CORDON BLEU SOUP

	PREP	PER SERVING
	30min	Serving: **1 cup**
x6	COOK	Calories: **178**
	6hours	Carbs:
		2.75 net grams
		Fat: **12 g**
		Protein: **16 g**

In the winter months, my slow cooker is my favorite kitchen appliance. I love that with the right ingredients, and a little preparation, you can develop such rich, complex flavors. This soup is a great make ahead to take to a party or to freeze in smaller batches to eat later. You are sure to love this soup version of an old classic.

INGREDIENTS (16 Servings)

- ☐ **6 Cups Chicken Broth**
- ☐ **12 oz. Ham** (Diced)
- ☐ **5 oz. Mushrooms** (Chopped)
- ☐ **4 oz. Onion** (Diced)
- ☐ **2 tsp. Tarragon**
- ☐ **1 tsp. Sea Salt** (More if desired)
- ☐ **1 tsp. Black Pepper**
- ☐ **1 lb. Chicken Breast** (Trimmed of fat and cubed)
- ☐ **3 Tbs. Garlic** (Minced)
- ☐ **3 Tbs. Salted Butter**
- ☐ **1 1/2 Cup Heavy Cream**
- ☐ **1/2 Cup Sour Cream**
- ☐ **1/2 Cup Parmesan Cheese** (Grated)
- ☐ **4 oz. Swiss Cheese**
- ☐ (2 Tbs. Peace and Love)

DIRECTIONS

1. Heat slow cooker on low setting.

2. To slow cooker, add chicken broth, diced ham, chopped mushrooms, onion, tarragon, salt and pepper. Cover and let cook.

3. In a large sauté pan, over medium-high heat, pan-sear cubed chicken in butter and garlic, until browned. Add chicken, along with all drippings from the pan to slow cooker.

4. Next, add heavy cream, sour cream, Parmesan cheese, and Swiss cheese. Cover and cook on low for 6 hours.

CREAMY TURKEY TACO SOUP

PREP
30min

COOK
6hours

PER SERVING

Serving:

About 1 cup

Calories: **178**

Carbs: **6 net g**

Fat: **10 g**

Protein: **4.5 g**

This soup is creamy and delicious. This is a great make ahead because it is even better when reheated the next day. You can substantially lower the carb count in this recipe simply by omitting the black beans. It tastes wonderful garnished with sharp cheddar cheese and sour cream.

INGREDIENTS (15 Servings)

- [ ] **1 - 15 oz. can Black Beans** (Drained)
- [ ] **1 - 14.5 oz. can Mexican Seasoned Stewed Tomatoes**
- [ ] **1 - 10 oz. can Tomatoes and Green Chilies**
- [ ] **28 oz. Beef Broth**
- [ ] **3 Cloves Garlic** (Minced)
- [ ] **20 oz. Ground Turkey**
- [ ] **3/4 Cup Sweet Onion** (Diced)
- [ ] **2 Tbs. Cumin**
- [ ] **1 tsp. Chili Powder**
- [ ] **1 1/2 tsp. Sea Salt**
- [ ] **8 oz. Cream Cheese** (Softened)
- [ ] **1 Cup Heavy Cream**
- [ ] (2 Tbs. Peace and Love)

DIRECTIONS

1. Heat slow cooker on low setting.

2. Add black beans, stewed tomatoes with juice, tomatoes and green chilies with juice, beef broth, and garlic. Cover and cook on low.

3. In a large sauté pan over medium-high heat, combine ground turkey, onion, cumin, chili powder, and sea salt. Sauté until turkey is cooked all the way through—about 15 minutes.

4. Reduce heat to low, add cream cheese to pan and mix until completely combined with turkey mixture.

5. Add turkey mixture and heavy cream to slow cooker. Stir until all ingredients are well incorporated. Cover and cook on low for 6-8 hours.

BALSAMIC FLAT IRON STEAK SALAD

 PREP 15min

COOK 30min

PER SERVING

Calories: **451**

Carbs: **10 net g**

Fat: **26 g**

Protein: **35 g**

This salad is so flavorful that it doesn't even require dressing. I love flat iron steak. It is a tender, underrated, affordable cut of meat. If time allows, soak the meat in the balsamic vinegar in the refrigerator overnight for added flavor.

INGREDIENTS (4 Servings)

- ☐ **1 1/2 lbs. Flat Iron Steak**
- ☐ **1/4 Cup Balsamic Vinegar**
- ☐ **3 Tbs. Olive Oil**
- ☐ **6 oz. Sweet Onion** (Sliced)
- ☐ **4 oz. Cremini Mushrooms** (Sliced)
- ☐ **2 Cloves Garlic** (Minced)
- ☐ **1 Large Head Romaine Lettuce** (Chopped)
- ☐ **1 Avocado** (Peeled, Pitted, and Sliced)
- ☐ **1 Orange Bell Pepper** (Sliced)
- ☐ **1 Yellow Bell Pepper** (Sliced)
- ☐ **3 oz. Sun-Dried Tomatoes**
- ☐ **1 tsp. Garlic Salt**
- ☐ **1 tsp. Onion Powder**
- ☐ **1 tsp. Italian Seasoning**
- ☐ **1 tsp. Red Pepper Flakes**
- ☐ (2 Tbs. Peace and Love)

DIRECTIONS

1. Slice flat iron steak into 1/2 inch thick slices. In a large mixing bowl, toss meat in balsamic vinegar, making sure that the pieces are evenly coated. Refrigerate.

2. In a large sauté pan, heat olive oil over low-medium heat. Once the pan is heated, add mushrooms, onion, garlic and a dash of salt and pepper. Sauté onions and mushrooms until caramelized—about 20 minutes.

3. In a large mixing bowl, combine chopped romaine, avocado, bell peppers, and sun-dried tomatoes.

4. On a lightly oiled broiling pan, line strips of steak in a single layer.

5. Combine garlic salt, onion powder, Italian seasoning and red pepper flakes. Sprinkle seasoning mixture over top of meat.

6. Broil on high on the top rack for 5-8 minutes, depending on preferred meat temperature.

7. Plate your salad mixture and pile on the caramelized onions, mushrooms and flat iron strips.

CUCUMBER GREEK SALAD

PREP
15min

COOK
None

PER SERVING

Calories: **246**

Protein: **9.5 g**

Carbs: **9 net g**

Fat: **17.5 g**

This Greek salad is great served as a complete meal or even as a starter before a meal. You can also serve it skewered as an antipasto appetizer. I love how all the rich flavored ingredients in this recipe come together so nicely. When I prepare this salad, I top it with Balsamic Shallot Vinaigrette. You can find that recipe on page 89.

INGREDIENTS (6 Servings)

- ☐ **2 Large Cucumbers** (Halved Lengthwise and Sliced)
- ☐ **1 Avocado** (Peeled, Pitted, and Cubed)
- ☐ **1/2 Cup Raw Cashews**
- ☐ **1/2 Cup Kalamata Olives**
- ☐ **1/2 Cup Sun-Dried Tomatoes**
- ☐ **1 1/2 oz. Red Onion** (Rough Chopped)
- ☐ **1/2 Cup Feta Cheese** (Crumbled)
- ☐ **4 oz. Peppered Salami** (Cut into strips)
- ☐ (2 Tbs. Peace and Love)

DIRECTIONS

1. In a large mixing bowl, combine cucumbers, avocado, cashews, kalamata olives, sun-dried tomatoes, red onion, feta cheese, and salami.

2. Toss with vinaigrette before serving.

STRAWBERRY SPINACH SALAD

PREP
15min

COOK
5min

PER SERVING

Calories: **255**

Protein: **14 g**

Carbs: **8 net g**

Fat: **16 g**

Once I had my first salad with fruit incorporated into it, I was instantly hooked. Strawberries are my favorite fruit to mix into salads. The bacon in this recipe gives this salad the perfect blend of sweet and salty. I serve this with the Balsamic Shallot Vinaigrette on Page 89.

INGREDIENTS (4 Servings)

- ☐ **10 oz. Fresh Spinach Leaves**
- ☐ **6 Slices Thick Cut Bacon** (Cooked Crisp and Crumbled)
- ☐ **2 Roma Tomatoes** (Diced)
- ☐ **4 oz. Feta Cheese** (Crumbled)
- ☐ **2 oz. Almonds**
- ☐ **2 oz. Red Onion** (Thinly Sliced)
- ☐ **8 Strawberries** (Sliced)
- ☐ (2 Tbs. Peace and Love)

DIRECTIONS

1. In a large mixing bowl, combine spinach, bacon, tomatoes, feta cheese, almonds, red onion, and strawberries. Toss until all ingredients are well mixed.

CHAPTER 3

BREAKFAST

CHEESY CHORIZO BREAKFAST BAKE

PREP
15min

COOK
1hour

PER SERVING

Calories: **292**

Carbs: **5 net g**

Fat: **23 g**

Protein: **17 g**

Chorizo is a great way to spice up breakfast. There are many different types of chorizo. For this recipe I used a Mexican pork chorizo. Mexican chorizo is not pre-cooked and typically comes in a casing. You will need to remove the casing before cooking. Also, certain brands of chorizo tend to be very salty. Make sure to taste it after it is cooked before adding additional salt.

INGREDIENTS (8 Servings)

- ☐ **2 Tbs. Butter**
- ☐ **4 oz. Onion** (Thinly sliced)
- ☐ **2 Tbs. Garlic** (Minced)
- ☐ **9 oz. Pork Chorizo**
- ☐ **4 oz. Cremini Mushrooms** (Sliced)
- ☐ **4 oz. Cream Cheese**
- ☐ **6 Eggs**
- ☐ **2/3 Cup Sharp Cheddar Cheese** (Shredded)
- ☐ **1/2 Cup Parmesan Cheese** (Grated)
- ☐ **Salt and Pepper** (To taste)
- ☐ (**2 Tbs. Peace and Love**)

DIRECTIONS

1. In a large sauté pan over low-medium heat, add butter, onion, garlic, and salt and pepper. Cook until onions are nice and caramelized—about 30 minutes.

2. At the same time, in a second sauté pan, over medium heat, add the chorizo and mushrooms. Cook until chorizo is cooked all the way through and the mushrooms are tender.

3. Drain excess grease from chorizo, reduce heat to low and mix in cream cheese. Add chorizo mixture to the caramelized onions and mix until all ingredients are well incorporated.

4. Into a large mixing bowl, crack the eggs and fork whisk. To the eggs, mix in sharp cheddar and Parmesan cheeses.

5. Preheat oven to 350°.

6. In an 8 x 8 glass baking dish, layer chorizo mixture into the bottom and spread evenly. Pour the egg mixture on top of the chorizo. Use a fork to poke holes down into the chorizo layer to allow the eggs to mix just slightly into the chorizo.

7. Bake uncovered on the middle rack for 30 minutes.

TIP: I like to garnish this dish with a dollop of sour cream and chopped green onions. (Nutritional values do not reflect these)

"POTATOES" O'BRIEN

 PREP
15min

 COOK
20min

PER SERVING

Calories: **74**

Carbs: **5 net g**

Fat: **5 g**

Protein: **1 g**

BREAKFAST

I love crisp, pan-fried breakfast potatoes. Potatoes O'Brien was one of my old carb-laden favorites. So, I decided to create a low-carb version of an old classic. Rutabagas are an excellent substitute for potatoes. They have a sweet and slightly bitter taste. But when combined with other ingredients, you can easily trick your palate into believing that you are actually eating potatoes.

INGREDIENTS (6 Servings)

- ☐ **1 Large Rutabaga** (Diced)
- ☐ **4 oz. Onion** (Diced)
- ☐ **1 oz. Red Bell Pepper** (Diced)
- ☐ **1 oz. Yellow Bell Pepper** (Diced)
- ☐ **1 oz. Orange Bell Pepper** (Diced)
- ☐ **2 Cloves Garlic** (Minced)
- ☐ **2 Tbs. Olive Oil**
- ☐ **Salt and Pepper** (To taste)
- ☐ (2 Tbs. Peace and Love)

DIRECTIONS

1. Clean, peel and dice the rutabaga. Try to dice all vegetables the same size. This way they will cook evenly.

2. In a large nonstick skillet, heat olive oil over medium-high heat. Once oil is heated, add rutabaga, onion, peppers, garlic and salt and pepper. Cook until all vegetables are tender—about 20 minutes.

SPICY SAUSAGE BREAKFAST TAQUITOS

PREP
30min

COOK
40min

PER SERVING
Per Serving:
2 Pieces
Calories: **589**
Protein: **32 g**
Carbs: **9.75 net g**
Fat: **46 g**

These taquitos are easy to make and will instantly have you hooked. You can make them with any of your favorite low-carb meats, vegetables or cheeses. They are delicious served with sour cream and salsa on the side.

INGREDIENTS (4 Servings)

- [ ] **4 Tbs. Butter** (Divided)
- [ ] **1/3 Cup Yellow Bell Peppers** (Chopped)
- [ ] **1/4 Cup Onion** (Chopped)
- [ ] **3 Baby Bella Mushrooms** (Chopped)
- [ ] **8 oz. Hot Italian Breakfast Sausage**
- [ ] **6 Large Eggs**
- [ ] **1/4 Cup Salsa**
- [ ] **4 Large Low Carb Tortillas**
- [ ] **1 Cup Sharp White Cheddar Cheese** (Shredded)
- [ ] **1/2 tsp. Onion Salt**
- [ ] **1/2 tsp. Italian Seasoning**
- [ ] (2 Tbs. Peace and Love)

DIRECTIONS

1. Preheat oven to 400°. Lightly oil or butter a baking sheet.

2. In a large sauté pan over medium heat, add 2 Tbs. butter, peppers, onion, mushrooms, and salt and pepper to taste. Sauté until tender.

3. In a separate pan, over medium heat, brown the sausage. Once the sausage is cooked all the way through, drain excess grease, and combine with vegetables.

4. In a large mixing bowl, combine eggs and salsa, and fork whisk.

5. Add egg mixture to the meat/vegetable mixture and cook until the eggs are scrambled.

6. Lay the tortillas flat and put a layer of cheese down the center of each one. Next, layer 1/4 of the scramble mixture down the center of each one. Top each one with another layer of cheese.

7. Roll tortillas tightly, packing the ends with any extra scramble mixture. Place on baking sheet, fold side down.

8. Melt remaining 2 Tbs. of butter and brush on top of the rolled tortillas. Combine onion salt and Italian seasoning and sprinkle the top of each tortilla.

9. Bake on the top rack 10-12 minutes. Flip each roll over, give another light brushing of melted butter and cook for 10-12 minutes more or until nice and crispy on both sides. Allow to cool and cut each one in half before serving.

CINNAMON VANILLA PANCAKES

PREP
15min

COOK
15min

PER SERVING

Calories: **255**

Protein: **9.2 g**

Carbs: **4.5 net g**

Fat: **22 g**

There is something so comforting about having pancakes on a cold winter morning. With this recipe you can continue to have them without spoiling your low-carb diet. I like to top mine with natural almond butter and sugar-free syrup.

INGREDIENTS (6 Servings)

- ☐ **2 Cups Low Carb Bake Mix**
- ☐ **3/4 Cup Half & Half**
- ☐ **1/3 Cup Water**
- ☐ **1 Egg**
- ☐ **1 Stick Salted Butter** (Melted)
- ☐ **3oz. Cream Cheese** (Softened)
- ☐ **4 Tbs. Sugar-Free Vanilla Syrup**
- ☐ **1 1/2 tsp. Cinnamon**
- ☐ (2 Tbs. Peace and Love)

DIRECTIONS

1. In a large mixing bowl, combine all ingredients. Using a hand mixer, mix all ingredients until well incorporated.

2. Heat a lightly oiled griddle or nonstick pan over medium heat.

3. Once the oil is heated, ladle a scoop of batter onto the griddle or pan. Once bubbles start to appear in the batter, it is time to flip. Brown on both sides.

BACON WRAPPED SCOTCH EGGS

PREP
20min

COOK
30min

PER SERVING

Calories: **423**

Protein: **26 g**

Carbs: **2 net g**

Fat: **35 g**

When I make these Scotch eggs, I like to grill asparagus in the bacon drippings and serve them with a side of Hollandaise sauce. It is a great way to make a meal out of it. The acidity of the Hollandaise sauce complements the savory flavors of the Scotch eggs perfectly.

INGREDIENTS (6 Servings)

- ☐ **1 lb. Ground Pork Sausage**
- ☐ **6 Slices Thick Cut Bacon**
- ☐ **6 Large Eggs**
- ☐ **1 Cup Sharp Cheddar Cheese** (Shredded)
- ☐ (2 Tbs. Peace and Love)

DIRECTIONS

1. Fill a medium sauce pan with cold water and place the eggs in the water. Bring water to a rolling boil over high heat. Remove pan from heat, cover and let sit for 10 minutes. Run eggs under cold water and peel.

2. Preheat oven to 400°.

3. In a large mixing bowl, combine sausage and cheese. Divide mixture into 6 equal portions. Flatten the portions out into patties.

4. Place an egg on top of each sausage patty and form the sausage around the egg until it is completely covered.

5. Place a cooling rack on top of a baking sheet and line your strips of bacon on it. Place the sausage wrapped eggs on the rack also. Bake for 30 Minutes on the middle rack.

6. Wrap each Scotch egg with a strip of bacon before serving.

SWEET POTATO & CHICKEN SAUSAGE HASH

PREP
15min

COOK
30min

PER SERVING

Calories: **214**

Carbs: **8 net g**

Fat: **13.5 g**

Protein: **11.5 g**

This hash is the perfect blend of sweet and savory. You can even add eggs to it and make a one pot wonder breakfast scramble.

INGREDIENTS (6 Servings)

- ☐ **1 Large Sweet Potato** (Diced)
- ☐ **3 oz. Yellow Bell Pepper** (Diced)
- ☐ **3 oz. Red Bell Pepper** (Diced)
- ☐ **2 Cloves Garlic** (Minced)
- ☐ **1 lb. Chicken Sausage**
- ☐ **5 oz. Onion** (Diced)
- ☐ **4 Tbs. Olive Oil** (Divided)
- ☐ **Salt and Pepper** (To taste)
- ☐ **1 Large Green Onion** (chopped)
- ☐ (2 Tbs. Peace and Love)

DIRECTIONS

1. In a large nonstick skillet, heat 2 Tbs. olive oil over medium-high heat. Once pan is hot, add sweet potatoes, peppers and garlic. Cook until sweet potatoes are tender and browned.

2. While the sweet potatoes are cooking, heat a second large skillet with 2 Tbs. olive oil over medium-high heat.

3. Once oil is heated, add chicken sausage, onion, and salt and pepper. Cook until the chicken sausage is no longer pink and the onions are translucent and soft.

4. Combine the ingredients of both pans. Garnish with green onions and serve.

SPICY SAUSAGE & CARAMELIZED ONION BREAKFAST BAKE

PREP
45min

COOK
40min

PER SERVING

Calories: **414**

Carbs: **5 net g**

Fat: **32 g**

Protein: **24 g**

This is probably one of my all-time favorite breakfasts. I think my husband would agree. Even though it says it is 8 servings, it will usually only last two days in our home as we typically end up eating for breakfast and dinner. I hope you enjoy it as much as we do.

INGREDIENTS (8 Servings)

- ☐ **1 Medium Onion** (Diced)
- ☐ **2 Tbs. Butter**
- ☐ **3 Tbs. Garlic** (Minced)
- ☐ **1lb. Hot Italian Breakfast Sausage**
- ☐ **8 oz. Mushrooms** (Sliced)
- ☐ **3 Tbs. Tomato Paste**
- ☐ **1 Tbs. Hot Sauce**
- ☐ **10 Large Eggs**
- ☐ **1 Cup Sharp Cheddar Cheese** (Shredded)
- ☐ **2/3 Cup Parmesan Cheese** (Grated)
- ☐ **Salt and Pepper** (To Taste)
- ☐ (2 Tbs. Peace and Love)

DIRECTIONS

1. In a large sauté pan over low-medium heat, add onion, butter, garlic, and salt and pepper. Cook until onions are nice and caramelized—about 30 minutes.

2. While the onions are cooking—in a large skillet, brown the sausage. Once the sausage is nearly finished cooking, add mushrooms, tomato paste, and hot sauce, and sauté 5-10 more minutes. Mix caramelized onions into meat mixture.

3. In a large mixing bowl, crack all 10 eggs and fork whisk. To the eggs, mix in cheddar cheese and Parmesan cheese.

4. Preheat oven to 350°.

5. In a 2 quart glass baking dish, pour meat into the bottom of the dish and spread evenly. Pour egg mixture over the top of the meat. Use a fork to poke holes down into the meat to allow the egg to mix just slightly into the meat.

6. Bake for 40 minutes. Once finished, the top should be a nice golden brown color.

TIP: I add a dollop of sour cream on top when I serve it. (The sour cream is not counted in the nutritional information.)

BALSAMIC FLAT IRON STEAK AND EGGS

PER SERVING

Calories: **585**

Protein: **52 g**

Carbs: **8.5 net g**

Fat: **34g**

This recipe was created as a result of using leftovers. I had left over steak from a steak salad and I thought I might try pairing it with eggs. While the idea of balsamic vinegar and eggs didn't quite sound appealing, the dish turned out amazing.

INGREDIENTS (4 Servings)

- ☐ **1 1/2 lb. Flat Iron Steak**
- ☐ **1/4 Cup Balsamic Vinegar**
- ☐ **2 Tbs. Olive Oil**
- ☐ **1 Large Onion** (Thinly Sliced)
- ☐ **8 oz. Mushrooms** (Sliced)
- ☐ **2 Tbs. Garlic** (Minced)
- ☐ **12 Eggs**
- ☐ **1/4 Cup Sour Cream**
- ☐ **1 tsp. Garlic Salt**
- ☐ **1 tsp. Onion Powder**
- ☐ **1 tsp. Italian Seasoning**
- ☐ **1 tsp. Red Pepper Flakes**
- ☐ (2 Tbs. Peace and Love)

DIRECTIONS

1. Slice flat iron steak into 1/2 inch thick slices. In a large mixing bowl, combine meat and balsamic vinegar. Toss the meat in the balsamic so that it covers all of the pieces. Set aside.

2. In a large sauté pan, heat olive oil over low-medium heat. Once your pan is heated, add onion, mushrooms, garlic and a dash of salt and pepper. Sauté until onions and mushrooms are nice and caramelized—about 20 minutes.

3. In a large mixing bowl, crack eggs and fork whisk with sour cream.

4. In a large nonstick pan, over medium heat, scramble the eggs. Using a rubber spatula, stir occasionally until eggs reach desired consistency.

5. Line strips of meat in a single layer on a broiling pan.

6. Combine garlic salt, onion powder, Italian seasoning and red pepper flakes. Sprinkle seasoning mixture over top of meat.

7. Broil on high on the top rack for 5 minutes (This will be medium-rare) Cook longer if you like your meat more on the well-done side.

8. Plate the eggs and pile on the caramelized onions, and mushrooms. Top with balsamic steak strips.

THE "EVERYTHING" STUFFED PEPPERS

PREP 30min

COOK 30min

PER SERVING

Calories: **420**

Protein: **29 g**

Carbs: **6.5 net g**

Fat: **29 g**

I initially called this dish "Kitchen Sink" Stuffed Peppers because they have everything but the kitchen sink in them. For the bell peppers in this recipe I used one each of green, red, yellow and orange. I love how colorful it made this dish. If you do not like fried eggs, you can always cook your eggs stove-top in any manner desired and then top the peppers with them.

INGREDIENTS (4 Servings)

- ☐ **4 Bell Peppers**
- ☐ **8 Large Eggs**
- ☐ **4 Strips Bacon** (Diced)
- ☐ **4 oz. Canadian Bacon** (Diced)
- ☐ **4 oz. Italian Breakfast Sausage**
- ☐ **5 Baby Bella Mushrooms** (Chopped)
- ☐ **1/2 Cup Sweet Onion** (Diced)
- ☐ **1 Tbs. Garlic** (Minced)
- ☐ **1 Cup Sharp White Cheddar Cheese** (Shredded)
- ☐ **Salt and Pepper** (To Taste)
- ☐ (2 Tbs. Peace and Love)

DIRECTIONS

1. Preheat oven to 275°.

2. Cut the peppers into halves—remove ribs and seeds

3. Put the peppers on a baking sheet and give them a light brushing of olive oil. Sprinkle each bell pepper with a little salt and pepper. Heat peppers in the oven while you prepare the rest of the ingredients.

4. In a large nonstick pan over medium-high heat, add bacon, Canadian bacon and sausage. Cook until all of the meats are fully cooked and crispy—about 15 minutes. Drain excess grease.

5. To the meat, add mushrooms, onion, and garlic. Continue to cook until the vegetables are tender. About 10 minutes.

6. Remove peppers from the oven, spoon meat mixture into cups, and top each pepper with cheese.

7. Using a spoon, press down in the center of each pepper cup to create a reservoir for the egg yolk. If you skip this step your eggs will just slide right off.

8. Crack an egg over the top of each pepper cup. Bake on the middle rack at 325° until the egg whites are cooked all the way through and the yolks have reached your desired consistency.

BACON SWEET POTATO CAKES

PREP
20min

COOK
40min

PER SERVING

Serving: **1 Cake**

Calories: **97**

Protein: **5 g**

Carbs: **4.6 net g**

Fat: **6 g**

I love to serve these sweet potato cakes with some sharp cheddar cheese, a dollop of sour cream and a medium poached egg on top.

INGREDIENTS (10 Servings)

- ☐ **1 Medium Head Cauliflower**
- ☐ **1 Medium Sweet Potato** (Grated)
- ☐ **5 Slices Thick Cut Bacon** (Cooked, and Crumbled)
- ☐ **2/3 Cup Almond Flour**
- ☐ **1/4 Cup Green Onions** (Chopped)
- ☐ **2 Large Eggs**
- ☐ **2 Cloves Garlic** (Minced)
- ☐ **1 tsp. Sea Salt**
- ☐ **1/2 tsp. Black Pepper**
- ☐ (2 Tbs. Peace and Love)

DIRECTIONS

1. Grate cauliflower or pulse in a food processor until it resembles rice. In a covered, microwave safe bowl, microwave cauliflower for 5 minutes.

2. In a large mixing bowl, combine cauliflower, sweet potato, bacon, almond flour, green onions, eggs, garlic, salt and pepper. Mix until all ingredients are well incorporated.

3. Heat oil in a large non-stick skillet, over medium heat. Once hot, take a scoop of the sweet potato mixture, form it into a patty and put it in the pan. Using a spatula, flatten it out, being careful not to separate it. Cook a few at a time. You may need to add fresh oil in between batches. Cook until browned on both sides—about 3 minutes each side.

4. Preheat oven to 350°. Line a baking sheet with parchment paper.

5. Place potato cakes on the baking sheet and finish in the oven. Bake for 20 minutes on middle rack.

CHAPTER 4

MAIN DISHES

PHILLY CHEESESTEAK STUFFED PEPPERS

PREP
15min

COOK
50min

PER SERVING

Calories: **458**

Protein: **27 g**

Carbs: **8.5 net g**

Fat: **36 g**

I'm not going to lie, when this idea came to me, I felt like a culinary genius. If you can't tell by now, I like finding creative vessels for my dishes. I have had a lot of fun with avocados with this same concept. These peppers are great for lunch, dinner or even as an appetizer. I hope you enjoy them as much as we have.

INGREDIENTS (4 Servings)

- ☐ **8 oz. Roast Beef** (Thinly Sliced)
- ☐ **8 Slices Provolone Cheese**
- ☐ **2 Large Green Bell Peppers**
- ☐ **1 Medium Sweet Onion** (Sliced)
- ☐ **6 oz. Baby Bella Mushrooms** (Sliced)
- ☐ **2 Tbs. Butter**
- ☐ **2 Tbs. Olive Oil**
- ☐ **1 Tbs. Garlic** (Minced)
- ☐ **Salt and Pepper** (to taste)
- ☐ (2 Tbs. Peace and Love)

DIRECTIONS

1. Slice peppers in half lengthwise, remove ribs and seeds.

2. In a large sauté pan over low-medium heat, add butter, olive oil, garlic, mushrooms, onion and a little salt and pepper. Sauté until onions and mushroom are nice and caramelized. About 30 minutes.

3. Preheat oven to 400°.

4. Slice roast beef into thin strips and add to the onion/mushroom mixture. Allow to cook 5-10 minutes.

5. Line the inside of each pepper with a slice of provolone cheese. Fill each pepper with meat mixture until they are nearly overflowing. Top each pepper with another slice of provolone cheese.

6. Bake for 15-20 minutes until the cheese on top is golden brown.

PORTOBELLO CORDON BLEU WITH DIJON CREAM SAUCE

PREP
15min

COOK
30min

PER SERVING

Calories: **402**

Protein: **15 g**

Carbs: **5 net g**

Fat: **25 g**

This dish turned out amazing and is one of those dishes that is even better the next day. My immediate thought upon tasting this was that if I slapped a poached egg on it, it would be an incredible breakfast dish. To make it gluten free, simply omit the panko. Or alternately you can substitute grated Parmesan cheese or crushed pork rinds. This will also lower the carb count.

INGREDIENTS (6 Servings)

- ☐ **6 Large Portobello Mushrooms**
- ☐ **3 Tbs. Olive Oil**
- ☐ **2 Tbs. Butter**
- ☐ **2 Tbs. Garlic** (Minced)
- ☐ **1 Cup Heavy Cream**
- ☐ **1/2 Cup Chicken Broth**
- ☐ **2 Tbs. Fresh Parsley** (Chopped)
- ☐ **1/4 Cup Parmesan Cheese** (Grated)
- ☐ **2 Tbs. Dijon Mustard**
- ☐ **8 oz. Ham** (Sliced)
- ☐ **6 Slices Swiss Cheese** (6oz.)
- ☐ **2 Tbs. Panko**
- ☐ **Salt and Pepper** (To Taste)
- ☐ (2 Tbs. Peace and Love)

DIRECTIONS

1. Preheat oven to 400° Line a baking sheet with aluminum foil.

2. Remove the stems from mushroom caps and slice a thin layer off of the top of the mushroom cap to allow it to sit flat. (Keep these pieces)

3. Brush mushrooms with olive oil and sprinkle with a little salt and pepper. Bake for 12 minutes.

4. Chop the mushroom stem and cap pieces that were trimmed in the first step.

5. In a large sauté pan, over medium heat, sauté chopped mushrooms in butter, and garlic for 5 minutes.

6. Add heavy cream, chicken broth and parsley to pan. Allow to come to a boil over medium heat and then reduce heat to low. Add Parmesan cheese and Dijon mustard to sauce. Simmer on low, stirring occasionally and allow sauce to thicken.

7. Pull mushrooms from oven. Fill caps with sauce, layer with ham, Swiss cheese, ham, Swiss cheese. Top with another dollop of sauce and a thin layer of panko on top of the sauce.

8. Bake for 7 additional minutes at 400°. Then broil on high for 2-3 minutes to allow panko to crisp.

PIZZA POCKETS

PREP
10min

COOK
10min

PER SERVING

Calories: **288**

Protein: **22 g**

Carbs: **6 net g**

Fat: **18.5 g**

Using a low carb tortilla in this recipe is a great way to satisfy your craving for pizza without having a very carb heavy crust. You can use any meats, cheeses and vegetables that you would normally love on a pizza.

INGREDIENTS (4 Servings)

- ☐ **2 Large Low Carb Tortillas**
- ☐ **1 1/2 Cup Mozzarella Cheese** (Shredded)
- ☐ **2 Tbs. Parmesan Cheese** (Grated)
- ☐ **4 Tbs. Pizza Sauce**
- ☐ **3 oz. Pepperoni Slices**
- ☐ **3 oz. Canadian Bacon**
- ☐ **2 Tbs. Olive Oil**
- ☐ **1 tsp. Oregano**
- ☐ **1 tsp. Italian Seasoning**
- ☐ **1 tsp. Garlic Powder**
- ☐ (2 Tbs. Peace and Love)

DIRECTIONS

1. Preheat oven to 400°.
2. Warm each tortilla in the microwave for about 20-30 seconds to soften.
3. Spoon 1 Tbs. pizza sauce on one half of each tortilla.
4. Divide half of the mozzarella cheese between the two tortillas. Leave some of the cheese close to the outer edge of the tortilla. This will help you pinch them closed when you are finished with the fillings.
5. Divide the meats evenly between the two tortillas and place on top of the cheese.
6. Divide the remaining mozzarella cheese between the two tortillas and layer on top of the meat.
7. Spoon 1 Tbs. pizza sauce over top of the cheese on each tortilla.
8. Fold the tortillas closed and pinch the edges together. If you can't get them to stay all the way closed, do not worry as they will stick together and stay closed in the oven.
9. Brush 1Tbs. olive oil over top of each pizza pocket. On top of the olive oil, sprinkle the oregano, Italian seasoning, and garlic powder. Finish by sprinkling 1 Tbs. grated parmesan on top.
10. Bake for 10 minutes. The Parmesan will make a nice golden brown crust.

PESTO CHICKEN WRAPS

PREP
10min

COOK
15min

PER SERVING

Calories: **397**

Protein: **24.5 g**

Carbs: **4.25 net g**

Fat: **33.5 g**

These are very simple to make but they sure don't taste like it. If you can't have or don't like low carb tortillas, you can always just eat the chicken salad. When I make chicken for recipes like this I like to pan-sear the chicken in butter. It makes the chicken just slightly crispy on the outside and wonderfully juicy on the inside.

INGREDIENTS (4 Servings)

- ☐ **2 Large Low Carb Tortillas**
- ☐ **12 oz. Chicken Breast** (Cooked and Cubed)
- ☐ **4 Slices Thick Cut Bacon** (Cooked Crisp and Crumbled)
- ☐ **1 oz. Red Onion** (Chopped)
- ☐ **4 Strips Roasted Red Peppers**
- ☐ **1/2 Cup Mayonnaise**
- ☐ **2 Tbs. Pesto**
- ☐ (2 Tbs. Peace and Love)

DIRECTIONS

1. In a large mixing bowl, combine chicken, bacon, red onion, roasted red peppers, mayonnaise, and pesto. Mix until all ingredients are well incorporated. Divide mixture between the two tortillas. Wrap and cut in half.

TURKEY CLUB PINWHEELS

PREP
10min

COOK
10min

PER SERVING

Calories: **278**

Protein: **11.5 g**

Carbs: **6.5 net g**

Fat: **21 g**

Not only are pinwheels delicious, they are bright and colorful. As far as ingredients, the possibilities are endless.

INGREDIENTS (4 Servings)

- ☐ **2 Large Low Carb Tortillas**
- ☐ **12 Slices Deli Turkey**
- ☐ **6 Strips Thick Cut Bacon** (Cooked Crisp)
- ☐ **4 oz. Roasted Red Peppers**
- ☐ **2 oz. Cream Cheese** (Softened)
- ☐ **2 Tbs. Ranch Dressing**
- ☐ **1 Medium Avocado** (Peeled, Pitted and Sliced)
- ☐ (2 Tbs. Peace and Love)

DIRECTIONS

1. Combine cream cheese and ranch dressing and divide equally between the two tortillas. Spread evenly, covering one whole side of each tortilla.

2. Top each tortilla with half of the turkey, bacon, roasted red peppers, and avocado slices.

3. Roll up tightly, being careful not to squeeze the toppings out of the sides.

4. Wrap tightly in plastic wrap and refrigerate for 30 minutes or until the wraps are firm enough to slice.

SLOPPY JOE STUFFED PEPPERS

PREP
20min

COOK
45min

PER SERVING

Calories: **392**

Protein: **48.5 g**

Carbs: **11.75 net g**

Fat: **12.5 g**

As a kid, Sloppy Joe's were a staple in my home. We must have eaten them once a week. As a grown up, I never ate them, until one day I had the strangest craving for one. Thus, this healthier, adult version of a childhood favorite was born. It also happens to be a lot less messy when it isn't spilling out of a bun. Win, win!

INGREDIENTS (4 Servings)

- ☐ **2 Yellow Bell Peppers**
- ☐ **2 Orange Bell Peppers**
- ☐ **2 Tbs. Butter**
- ☐ **1 1/2 lb. Ground Beef**
- ☐ **3 oz. Onion** (Chopped)
- ☐ **2 oz. Carrots** (Chopped)
- ☐ **1 Rib Celery** (Chopped)
- ☐ **3 Large Cloves Garlic** (Minced)
- ☐ **8 oz. Can Zesty Tomato and Green Chili Sauce**
- ☐ **1/3 Cup Beef Broth**
- ☐ **1/4 Cup Reduced Sugar Ketchup**
- ☐ **2 Tbs. Tomato Paste**
- ☐ **1 Tbs. Worcestershire Sauce**
- ☐ **1 tsp. Yellow Mustard**
- ☐ **1 Tbs. Chili Powder**
- ☐ **1 tsp. Cumin**
- ☐ **1 tsp. Salt**
- ☐ (2 Tbs. Peace and Love)

DIRECTIONS

1. Preheat oven to 350°.

2. Rinse bell peppers, cut off tops and remove ribs and seeds from inside. Lightly grease a baking sheet with butter. Sprinkle peppers with a pinch of salt and pepper and place on baking sheet. Bake 35 minutes on middle rack.

3. In a large non-stick skillet, over medium-high heat, add ground beef, onion, carrots, celery, and garlic. Cook until ground beef is cooked through—about 10 minutes. Drain excess grease from pan.

4. To meat mixture, add tomato and green chili sauce, beef broth, ketchup, tomato paste, Worcestershire, mustard, chili powder, cumin, and salt. Mix until all ingredients are well incorporated. Reduce heat to low and simmer 5-10 minutes.

5. Once finished baking, remove peppers from oven and stuff with sloppy Joe mixture.

SLOPPY JOE STUFFED SWEET POTATOES

PREP
20min

COOK
45min

PER SERVING

Calories: **445**

Protein: **49.5 g**

Carbs: **18.75 net g**

Fat: **12.5 g**

This turned out to be the most delicious combination. I realize that many of you do not eat sweet potatoes as they have a higher carb count. While the nutritional information at the top reflects the sloppy Joe mixture as well as the sweet potato, at the bottom you will find the nutritional count for just the sloppy Joe mix.

INGREDIENTS (4 Servings)

- ☐ **2 Large Sweet Potatoes**
- ☐ **2 Tbs. Butter**
- ☐ **1 1/2 lb. Lean Ground Beef**
- ☐ **3 oz. Onion** (Chopped)
- ☐ **2 oz. Carrots** (Chopped)
- ☐ **1 Rib Celery** (Chopped)
- ☐ **3 Large Cloves Garlic** (Minced)
- ☐ **8 oz. Can Zesty Tomato and Green Chili Sauce**
- ☐ **1/3 Cup Beef Broth**
- ☐ **1/4 Cup Reduced Sugar Ketchup**
- ☐ **2 Tbs. Tomato Paste**
- ☐ **1 Tbs. Worcestershire Sauce**
- ☐ **1 tsp. Yellow Mustard**
- ☐ **1 Tbs. Chili Powder**
- ☐ **1 tsp. Cumin**
- ☐ **1 tsp. Salt**
- ☐ (2 Tbs. Peace and Love)

DIRECTIONS

1. Preheat oven to 350°.

2. Rinse sweet potatoes and cut in half lengthwise. Place cut side up on a foil lined baking sheet. Top each sweet potato with butter and sprinkle with salt and pepper. Bake 45 minutes.

3. In a large non-stick skillet, over medium-high heat, add ground beef, onion, carrots, celery, and garlic. Cook until ground beef is cooked through—about 10 minutes. Drain excess grease from pan.

4. To meat mixture, add tomato and green chili sauce, beef broth, ketchup, tomato paste, Worcestershire, mustard, chili powder, cumin, and salt. Mix until all ingredients are well incorporated. Reduce heat to low and simmer 5-10 minutes.

5. Once the sweet potatoes are finished baking, remove them from the oven. Run a fork over top of each sweet potato like a rake to loosen the potato. Top with sloppy Joe mixture.

NUTRITIONAL INFO (Sloppy Joe Mix Only)

Servings: **4**

Calories: **355**

Protein: **4 7.5 g**

Carbs: **7.75 net g**

Fat: **12.5 g**

CHICKEN CORDON BLEU CASSEROLE

PREP 15min

COOK 45min

PER SERVING

Calories: **383**

Protein: **32 g**

Carbs: **7 net g**

Fat: **24g**

Don't be discouraged by the multiple steps in this recipe. This casserole is worth it. It is a great make ahead meal and it freezes well. I would recommend reheating in the oven. This also makes for a great brunch side dish.

INGREDIENTS (8 Servings)

- ☐ **1 lb. Chicken Breast** (Trimmed of fat and cubed)
- ☐ **3 Tbs. Butter** (Salted)
- ☐ **1 Large Head Cauliflower** (Cleaned and trimmed)
- ☐ **1/2 Cup Chicken Broth**
- ☐ **12 oz. Ham** (Diced)
- ☐ **4 oz. Onion** (Chopped)
- ☐ **3 oz. Mushrooms** (Chopped)
- ☐ **1 1/4 Cup Heavy Cream**
- ☐ **1 Cup Parmesan Cheese** (Grated and Divided)
- ☐ **1/2 Cup Sour Cream**
- ☐ **3.5 oz. Swiss Cheese** (Divided)
- ☐ **1 tsp. Tarragon**
- ☐ **Salt and Pepper** (To taste)
- ☐ (2 Tbs. Peace and Love)

DIRECTIONS

1. Preheat oven to 350°

2. In large skillet over medium-high heat, brown chicken in 3 Tbs. Butter. Once chicken is browned on both sides, add ham, onion and mushrooms to pan. Reduce heat to medium and continue cooking until onions are translucent and soft.

3. At the same time, steam the head of cauliflower (whole) in chicken broth, in a covered sauce pot over high heat. Steam until cauliflower is fork tender. Drain chicken broth and leave cauliflower in hot pot. This will allow some of the excess moisture to evaporate. Once nearly all of the liquid is evaporated, fork mash the cauliflower.

4. In medium sauce pot, combine heavy cream, ½ cup Parmesan cheese, sour cream, 1.5 oz. Swiss cheese, tarragon and salt and pepper. Bring to a boil over medium-high heat and then reduce heat to low and simmer—about 10 minutes. Stir frequently.

5. In a 3 quart 9 x 9 casserole dish, combine cauliflower, meat mixture and sauce. Once all the ingredients are well incorporated, cover the top with remaining Swiss cheese and Parmesan cheese. Bake for 25 minutes.

PAN-SEARED CHICKEN WITH BALSAMIC CREAM SAUCE, MUSHROOMS AND ONIONS

PREP
20min

COOK
40min

PER SERVING

Calories: **482**

Protein: **42 g**

Carbs: **6.5 net g**

Fat: **33 g**

This recipe still reigns supreme as my all-time favorite. This chicken is like the kid who peaked in high school. It's all downhill from here. But in all seriousness, this dish has been quite the crowd pleaser. It is in heavy rotation in my home, and I hope it will be in yours as well.

INGREDIENTS (4 Servings)

- ☐ **1 Medium Onion** (Thinly sliced)
- ☐ **1 1/2 lb. Boneless, Skinless Chicken Breasts**
- ☐ **5 Tbs. Butter** (Divided)
- ☐ **1/2 Cup Chicken Broth**
- ☐ **1 Cup Heavy Cream**
- ☐ **2 Tbs. Balsamic Vinegar**
- ☐ **8 oz. Baby Bella Mushrooms** (Halved)
- ☐ **1/2 Cup Parmesan Cheese**
- ☐ **Salt and Pepper** (To Taste)
- ☐ (2 Tbs. Peace and Love)

DIRECTIONS

1. Lightly season the chicken breasts with salt and pepper on both sides.

2. In a large sauté pan over low-medium heat, add 2 Tbs. butter, onion and salt and pepper. Cook until onions are nice and caramelized—about 20 minutes. Remove from the heat and set aside.

3. In a separate pan, over medium-high heat, pan-sear the chicken breasts in remaining 3 Tbs. butter. Brown on both sides—remove from pan and set aside. (Chicken will not be fully cooking during this stage)

4. De-glaze the pan with chicken broth. Using a rubber spatula, scrape the pan and mix in any remaining bits of chicken. Let simmer 5 minutes.

5. Reduce heat to low, add heavy cream, balsamic vinegar, mushrooms and a little salt and pepper. Let simmer 10 minutes.

6. Add chicken breasts back to the sauce pan, and simmer until the chicken is cooked all the way through. About 10-15 minutes

7. Remove chicken breasts from the pan and plate. Add the Parmesan cheese and caramelized onions to the sauce and stir until the cheese is melted in to the sauce. Pour sauce over top of chicken.

BALSAMIC MUSTARD STEAKS

PREP
10min

COOK
25min

PER SERVING

Calories: **490**

Protein: **33 g**

Carbs: **4 net g**

Fat: **35 g**

This flavor combination really packs a punch. The spiciness of the mustard and the acidity of the balsamic come together nicely and make the perfect sauce to top an already delicious piece of meat.

INGREDIENTS (4 Servings)

- [ ] **1 1/2 lb. Steak** (The cut of your choice)
- [ ] **2 Tbs. Olive Oil**
- [ ] **1 Shallot** (Finely Chopped)
- [ ] **2 Tbs. Butter**
- [ ] **1/3 Cup Balsamic Vinegar**
- [ ] **1/4 Cup Beef Broth**
- [ ] **1/4 Cup Spicy Brown Mustard**
- [ ] **Salt and Pepper** (To Taste)
- [ ] (2 Tbs. Peace and Love)

DIRECTIONS

1. In a large skillet, heat olive oil over medium-high heat.
2. Season the steaks on both sides with a little salt and pepper.
3. Sear the steaks for 3-4 minutes on each side or until they have reached desired doneness. Remove the steaks from the pan, and place on a plate covered with foil while you make the sauce. Alternately you can hold the steaks in the oven on low.
4. To the skillet, add shallot and butter and sauté until soft and translucent. Add balsamic vinegar to pan. Use a rubber spatula to scrape any bits of steak from the bottom of the pan and mix into sauce. Bring to a boil over medium heat and then reduce heat to low and simmer 5 minutes.
5. Add beef broth and whisk in mustard. Simmer on low, stirring occasionally—about 10 minutes or until sauce has thickened.

PROSCIUTTO WRAPPED STUFFED CHICKEN WITH PESTO CREAM SAUCE

PREP
15min

COOK
30min

PER SERVING

Calories: **402**

Protein: **15 g**

Carbs: **5 net g**

Fat: **25 g**

There are so many different flavors going on in this dish. They all manage to play together nicely and create a rich, complex flavor. Chicken can become so boring after a short time. I like to create new ways to dress it up and give chicken it's proper time in the spotlight.

INGREDIENTS (6 Servings)

- ☐ **1 1/2 lbs. Boneless, Skinless Chicken Breasts** (4 Pieces)
- ☐ **6 Tbs. Butter** (Divided)
- ☐ **2 Tbs. Garlic** (Minced)
- ☐ **1/2 Cup Chicken Broth**
- ☐ **4 oz. Goat Cheese**
- ☐ **1/2 Cup Sun-Dried Tomatoes**
- ☐ **8 Large Slices of Prosciutto**
- ☐ **1 Cup Heavy Cream**
- ☐ **1/4 Cup Pesto**
- ☐ **1/2 Cup Parmesan Cheese** (Grated)
- ☐ **2 Tbs. Pine Nuts** (Toasted)
- ☐ **Salt and Pepper** (To taste)
- ☐ (2 Tbs. Peace and Love)

DIRECTIONS

1. Preheat oven to 350°

2. Lightly season the chicken breasts with salt and pepper on both sides.

3. In a large sauté pan, over medium-high heat, pan-sear the chicken breasts in 3 Tbs. butter. Brown on both sides—remove from pan and set aside. (Chicken will not be fully cooking during this stage)

4. Reduce heat to medium, add remaining 3 Tbs. butter and garlic to the pan. Sauté until the butter is browned and the garlic is aromatic – About 2 minutes. Be careful not to burn the garlic as it will taste very bitter.

5. De-glaze the pan with chicken broth. Using a rubber spatula, scrape the pan and mix in any remaining bits of chicken. Let simmer 5 minutes.

6. While the base of your sauce is simmering, cut slits lengthwise in the chicken breasts about three-quarters of the way in, creating a pocket in which to stuff the chicken. Divide the sun-dried tomatoes and goat cheese between the 4 breasts and stuff each one. After stuffing, wrap each breast tightly with 2 pieces of prosciutto.

7. Place chicken on a cooling rack on a baking sheet. Place in oven and bake 25 minutes. Doing this will allow the prosciutto to crisp up on both sides.

8. Now back to the sauce—to the pan add heavy cream, pesto and Parmesan cheese. Reduce heat to low and simmer for 10 minutes. Stir frequently so the sauce does not get too thick or stick to the bottom of the pan.

9. Plate chicken breast, top with sauce and garnish with toasted pine nuts.

CHILI LIME PRAWN SKEWERS

 PREP
15min

COOK
10min

PER SERVING

Calories: **190**

Protein: **24 g**

Carbs: **2.5 net g**

Fat: **4 g**

This recipe is so simple but you wouldn't know it by the taste. Chili lime is one of my favorite flavor combinations and marinating prawns in it is no exception. If you have time to make these several hours ahead of time, they will taste even better with the extra marinating time.

INGREDIENTS (4 Servings)

- ☐ **1 lb. 16/20 Prawns** (Cleaned and Deveined)
- ☐ **2 Cloves Garlic** (Minced)
- ☐ **2 Tbs. Soy Sauce**
- ☐ **2 Tbs. Olive Oil**
- ☐ **1 tsp. Chili Powder**
- ☐ **1/2 tsp. Onion Powder**
- ☐ **1 Lime** (Juiced and Zested)
- ☐ (2 Tbs. Peace and Love)

DIRECTIONS

1. In a large bowl, combine prawns, garlic, soy sauce, olive oil, chili powder, onion powder and the juice and zest of one lime. Allow to marinate in refrigerator for at least 1 hour.

2. Skewer prawns and grill over medium heat, using a grill pan or a barbecue—about 2-3 minutes per side. You will know the prawns are done when they turn nice and pink.

TIP: When you see numbers like 16/20 in reference to seafood, it is telling you the number of pieces per pound. So, in this case, you would be getting 16-20 prawns per pound.

LEMON GARLIC FLOUNDER

PREP
10min

COOK
15min

PER SERVING

Calories: **153**

Protein: **38 g**

Carbs: **2 net g**

Fat: **3 g**

Flounder is a very light fish with subtle flavor. If you are new to eating seafood or are not a huge fan of it, flounder is a good way to transition into adding more seafood into your diet. It does not have a strong fishy taste and is super easy to prepare.

INGREDIENTS (4 Servings)

- ☐ **1 1/2 lbs. Flounder**
- ☐ **3 Tbs. Garlic** (Minced)
- ☐ **1 Tbs. Lemon Pepper Seasoning**
- ☐ **1 tsp. Onion Salt**
- ☐ **1 tsp. Italian Seasoning**
- ☐ **1 Lemon** (Sliced)
- ☐ **2 Green Onions** (Chopped)
- ☐ (2 Tbs. Peace and Love)

DIRECTIONS

1. Preheat oven to 350° Line a baking sheet with aluminum foil.

2. Place flounder on foil and top each fillet with a little olive oil. Top each piece generously with garlic.

3. Combine lemon pepper seasoning, onion salt, and Italian seasoning and sprinkle over top of each fillet.

4. Top each piece with lemon slices and bake for 15 minutes.

5. Top with green onions before serving.

STUFFED PORK CHOPS WITH PEPPER JACK CREAM SAUCE

PREP
20min

COOK
45min

PER SERVING

Calories: **611**

Protein: **36 g**

Carbs: **8 net g**

Fat: **47 g**

This dish is not for the faint of heart. It is full of calories and delicious fat but comes in at just 8 net carbs for an entire dinner meal. You are sure to love this indulgent, restaurant quality meal.

INGREDIENTS (4 Servings)

PORK CHOPS

- ☐ **6 Thick Cut Boneless Pork Loin Chops**
- ☐ **4 Tbs. Butter** (Divided)
- ☐ **6 oz. Mushrooms** (Chopped)
- ☐ **1 Orange Bell Pepper** (Chopped)
- ☐ **1 Yellow Bell Pepper** (Chopped)
- ☐ **1 Red Bell Pepper** (Chopped)
- ☐ **1 Medium Onion** (Chopped)
- ☐ **2 Ribs Celery** (Chopped)
- ☐ **1 Shallot** (Diced)
- ☐ **2 Tbs. Garlic** (Minced)
- ☐ **Salt and Pepper** (To Taste)

SAUCE

- ☐ **1 Tbs. Garlic** (Minced)
- ☐ **4 Tbs. Butter**
- ☐ **1 Cup Heavy Cream**
- ☐ **1/2 Cup Pepper Jack Cheese** (Shredded)
- ☐ **1/2 Cup Parmesan Cheese** (Grated)
- ☐ **2 Tbs. Fresh Parsley** (Chopped)

DIRECTIONS

PORK CHOPS

1. Preheat oven to 300°. Lightly oil a baking sheet.
2. Season pork chops on both sides with a little salt and pepper.
3. In a large sauté pan, over medium-high heat, add 2 Tbs. butter and pork chops. Brown the chops on both sides until they are a nice caramel color—about 2 minutes each side. Remove from pan and set aside. (Chops will not be fully cooked at this stage.)
4. Reduce heat to medium, add remaining 2 Tbs. butter, mushrooms, bell peppers, onion, celery, shallot, garlic and a little salt and pepper to the pan. Sauté until vegetables are tender—about 10 minutes.
5. Cut slits in the pork chops lengthwise about three quarters of the way back, making a pocket in which to stuff the vegetables.
6. Stuff a heaping portion of the vegetable hash into each pork chop and place on baking sheet. There will be vegetables left over. Use this to plate under the chops or to serve on the side.
7. Bake for 15 minutes on the middle rack.

SAUCE

1. In a separate pan, over medium heat, sauté the butter and garlic until they are a nice golden brown color. (Be careful not to burn the garlic or it will become very bitter and ruin the taste of your sauce.)
2. Add heavy cream, reduce heat to low and simmer for 5 minutes. To the sauce, add pepper jack cheese, Parmesan cheese and parsley. Stir until cheese is completely melted. Simmer an additional 5 minutes and continue stirring.
3. Plate the remaining vegetables, place the pork chops on top, cover with the sauce.

AVOCADO TACO BOATS

PREP
15min

COOK
20min

PER SERVING

Calories: **384**

Protein: **31 g**

Carbs: **6 net g**

Fat: **26 g**

This is the recipe that started it all. It was the first recipe to garner a lot of attention on my site. It is also where my love affair with avocados began.

INGREDIENTS (6 Servings)

- ☐ **1 1/2 lb. Lean Ground Beef**
- ☐ **6 Tbs. Taco Seasoning** (Page 98)
- ☐ **1 Cup Water**
- ☐ **3 Large Avocados**
- ☐ **2 Tbs. Lime Juice**
- ☐ **2 Tbs. Dried Onion Flakes**
- ☐ **1/2 Cup Salsa** (Divided)
- ☐ **1 Cup Sharp Cheddar Cheese** (Shredded)
- ☐ **1/3 Cup Sour Cream**
- ☐ **6 Pickled Jalapeno Slices**
- ☐ **6 Grape Tomatoes** (Halved)
- ☐ **Salt and Pepper** (To Taste)
- ☐ (2 Tbs. Peace and Love)

DIRECTIONS

1. In a large skillet over medium-high heat, brown the ground beef. Once browned, drain excess grease from pan. Add taco seasoning and 1 cup water, reduce heat to low, and let simmer until sauce has thickened.

2. Cut the avocados in half lengthwise. Using a spoon, scoop out the avocado and discard the pits. Save the avocado shells as you will be using them later.

3. In a large bowl, combine avocado, lime juice, onion flakes, ¼ cup salsa and salt and pepper. Fork mash until all ingredients are well combined.

4. In the empty avocado shells, spoon in the guacamole mixture. Next, layer on taco meat, cheese, salsa, sour cream, jalapenos, and tomatoes.

GREEK PIZZA

PREP
15min

COOK
20min

PER SERVING

Calories: **89**

Protein: **4.5 g**

Carbs: **6 net g**

Fat: **6 g**

MAIN DISHES

For this recipe you must first prepare the Pizza Crust featured on page 100. You can make the crust on a pizza pan or in a 13x9 glass baking dish. Some other pizza variations I have made are chicken bacon ranch, supreme, and vegetarian.

INGREDIENTS (6 Servings)

- ☐ **1/4 Cup Pizza Sauce**
- ☐ **1/4 Cup Mozzarella Cheese** (Shredded)
- ☐ **12 Kalamata Olives**
- ☐ **1/2 Cup Quartered Artichoke Hearts**
- ☐ **1/2 Cup Fire Roasted Tomatoes**
- ☐ **1/3 Cup Red Onions** (Sliced)
- ☐ **1/2 Cup Feta Cheese** (Crumble)
- ☐ (2 Tbs. Peace and Love)

DIRECTIONS

1. Preheat oven to 350°.

2. After you have prepared your crust, pour on the pizza sauce and spread the sauce out to the edges of the crust. Top with mozzarella cheese.

3. Top the pizza with kalamata olives, artichoke hearts, fire-roasted tomatoes, and red onions. Crumble the feta over the top.

4. Bake for 20 minutes.

PEPPERONI PIZZA STUFFED PEPPERS

 PREP
15min

 COOK
40min

PER SERVING

Calories: **208**

Protein: **14 g**

Carbs: **6 net g**

Fat: **15 g**

This concept is so great because you can easily do it with any of your favorite pizza toppings. The peppers make a nice vessel to hold all of the toppings. I have done this in several different variations and it is always a crowd pleaser. Using 4 different colored peppers makes it visually stunning as well.

INGREDIENTS (8 Servings)

- ☐ **1 Large Orange Bell Pepper**
- ☐ **1 Large Yellow Bell Pepper**
- ☐ **1 Large Red Bell Pepper**
- ☐ **1 Large Green Bell Pepper**
- ☐ **8 oz. Mozzarella Cheese** (Shredded)
- ☐ **1 Cup Pizza Sauce**
- ☐ **4 oz. Pepperoni Slices**
- ☐ **1/2 Cup Parmesan Cheese**
- ☐ **1 tsp. Italian Seasoning**
- ☐ **OPTIONAL: 12 Black Olives** (Sliced)
- ☐ (2 Tbs. Peace and Love)

DIRECTIONS

1. Preheat oven to 400°. Line a baking sheet with aluminum foil.

2. Cut the bell peppers in half and remove the ribs and seeds. Place pepper halves on baking sheet and bake for 20 minutes on middle rack.

3. Layer each pepper cup with mozzarella cheese, sauce, pepperoni, and (olives). Then top each pepper cup with any remaining mozzarella, and sprinkle the top with Parmesan cheese and Italian Seasoning.

4. Bake 20 additional minutes or until Parmesan cheese on top is golden brown.

HAWAIIAN PIZZA STUFFED PEPPERS

PREP 15min

COOK 40min

PER SERVING

Calories: **187**

Protein: **17 g**

Carbs: **8.5 net g**

Fat: **11 g**

I love the way these Hawaiian pizza stuffed peppers taste with a garlic cream sauce as opposed to a red sauce. The savory flavor of the garlic balances out the sweetness of the pineapple. There is the added bonus that cream sauces are typically lower in carbs that red sauces.

INGREDIENTS (8 Servings)

- ☐ **1 Large Orange Bell Pepper**
- ☐ **1 Large Yellow Bell Pepper**
- ☐ **1 Large Red Bell Pepper**
- ☐ **1 Large Green Bell Pepper**
- ☐ **8 oz. Mozzarella Cheese** (Shredded)
- ☐ **1 Cup Low Carb Garlic Cream Sauce**
- ☐ **4 oz. Sliced Canadian Bacon**
- ☐ **8 oz. Canned Pineapple**
- ☐ **1/2 Cup Parmesan Cheese**
- ☐ **1 tsp. Italian Seasoning**
- ☐ (2 Tbs. Peace and Love)

DIRECTIONS

1. Preheat oven to 400°. Line a baking sheet with aluminum foil.

2. Cut the bell peppers in half and remove the ribs and seeds. Place pepper halves on baking sheet and bake for 20 minutes on middle rack.

3. Layer each pepper cup with mozzarella cheese, sauce, Canadian bacon and pineapple. Then top each pepper cup with any remaining mozzarella, and sprinkle the top with Parmesan cheese and Italian Seasoning.

4. Bake 20 additional minutes or until Parmesan cheese on top is golden brown.

CRISPY BUFFALO CHICKEN TENDERS

PREP
20min

COOK
20min

PER SERVING

Calories: **430**

Protein: **56 g**

Carbs: **7 net g**

Fat: **34 g**

I love to serve these with the Avocado Ranch Dressing featured on Page 85. The spiciness of the buffalo sauce and the cool taste of the ranch are a match made in heaven.

INGREDIENTS (4 Servings)

- ☐ **1 1/2 Boneless, Skinless Chicken Breasts**
- ☐ **2 Cups Spicy Buffalo Roasted Nuts** (Page 77)
- ☐ **2 Eggs**
- ☐ **1/2 tsp. Garlic Pepper Seasoning**
- ☐ **1/2 tsp. Salt**
- ☐ (2 Tbs. Peace and Love)

DIRECTIONS

1. Preheat oven to 350°. Line a baking sheet with parchment paper.

2. Trim fat from chicken breasts and cut into tenders sized pieces.

3. Pour the nuts in a food processor or blender and give a few quick pulses until the nuts are finely ground. Pour mixture onto a plate.

4. In a shallow mixing bowl, fork whisk eggs with garlic pepper seasoning, and salt.

5. Dredge chicken in egg wash, then press firmly into nut mixture, evenly and liberally coating both sides. Place breaded chicken on parchment paper. Repeat this process until all of the chicken is breaded.

6. Bake on the middle rack for 20 minutes.

TURKEY TACO MEATLOAF MUFFINS

PREP 15min

COOK 30min

PER SERVING

Calories: **445**

Protein: **23 g**

Carbs: **8 net g**

Fat: **20 g**

I can't tell you the last time I used a muffin tin to make actual muffins. I love that I can make pre-portioned meals and snacks with a muffin tin. They are also great for making breakfast muffins with eggs, meat and veggies. These turkey taco meatloaf muffins are another great make ahead meal. Take one with you, pop it in the microwave and in no time, you are ready to eat.

INGREDIENTS (4 Servings)

- ☐ **1 lb. Lean Ground Turkey**
- ☐ **4 Tbs. Taco Seasoning** (Page 98)
- ☐ **1/2 Cup Salsa**
- ☐ **1 Cup Sharp Cheddar Cheese** (Divided)
- ☐ **3 oz. Yellow Bell Peppers** (Diced)
- ☐ **1 Clove Garlic** (Minced)
- ☐ **2 Tbs. Dried Onion Flakes**
- ☐ **1 Roma Tomato** (Diced)
- ☐ **1 Medium Avocado**
- ☐ **1/2 Cup Sour Cream**
- ☐ **10 Black Olives** (Sliced)
- ☐ (2 Tbs. Peace and Love)

DIRECTIONS

1. Preheat oven to 350°.

2. In a large mixing bowl, combine ground turkey, taco seasoning, salsa, 1/2 cup cheddar cheese, bell peppers, garlic and onion flakes. Mix until all ingredients are well combined.

3. In a standard size muffin tin, fill 8 holes with the meat mixture. Bake for 25 minutes.

4. Remove each meatloaf muffin from the tin and top with remaining cheese, tomato, avocado, sour cream and olives.

BLACKENED DIJON CHICKEN

PREP
10min

COOK
30min

PER SERVING

Calories: **220**

Protein: **38 g**

Carbs: **1 net g**

Fat: **3 g**

This recipe came about by accident and turned into a household favorite. I like to serve this with a nice big portion of oven roasted vegetables and a side salad. It is one of my favorite dinners.

INGREDIENTS (4 Servings)

- ☐ **1 1/2 lbs. Boneless, Skinless Chicken Breasts**
- ☐ **1/4 Cup Dijon Mustard**
- ☐ **3 Tbs. Blackened Seasoning** (Page 97)
- ☐ (2 Tbs. Peace and Love)

DIRECTIONS

1. Preheat oven to 400°.
2. Coat each chicken breast liberally on both sides with blackened seasoning. Brush each side with Dijon mustard.
3. In a large, oiled skillet over medium-high heat, sear the chicken for 3 minutes on each side.
4. Remove chicken from pan and place on a baking sheet. Bake for 20 minutes.

BLACKENED PORK CHOPS WITH BALSAMIC PEPPERS AND ONIONS

PREP
15min

COOK
25min

PER SERVING

Calories: **528**

Protein: **47 g**

Carbs: **4 net g**

Fat: **34 g**

The spiciness of the blackened seasoning, the acidity of the balsamic vinegar and the sweetness of the caramelized onions come together perfectly in this dish to create the ultimate flavor trifecta. I love to serve these chops with the Caramelized Onion, Horseradish Cauliflower Mash featured on page 79.

INGREDIENTS (4 Servings)

- ☐ **1 Medium Onion** (Thinly Sliced)
- ☐ **2 Cloves Garlic** (Minced)
- ☐ **4 Tbs. Olive Oil** (Divided)
- ☐ **4 oz. Mixed Bell Peppers** (Sliced)
- ☐ **2 Tbs. Balsamic Vinegar**
- ☐ **4 Pork Loin Chops**
- ☐ **2 Tbs. Blackened Seasoning** (Page 97)
- ☐ **3 Tbs. Italian Flat Leaf Parsley** (Chopped)
- ☐ (2 Tbs. Peace and Love)

DIRECTIONS

1. Liberally coat each side of the pork chops with blackened seasoning and allow to rest 15 minutes.

2. In a large sauté pan over low-medium heat, sauté onion, and garlic in 2 Tbs. olive oil for 10 minutes.

3. Add peppers and balsamic to the pan, increase heat to medium and sauté and additional 6-8 minutes.

4. Over medium-high heat, in a large skillet or grill pan, heat remaining 2 Tbs. olive oil.

5. Place pork chops in pan and cook 3-4 minutes per side or until cooked through.

6. Top with peppers and onions and finish by garnishing with fresh parsley.

CREAMY CHICKEN SCAMPI

PREP
20min

COOK
30min

PER SERVING

Calories: **464**

Protein: **38 g**

Carbs: **4 net g**

Fat: **34 g**

I used to eat at a certain chain Italian restaurant all the time and their chicken scampi was one of my favorite things in the world. I decided to try and create it in a low carb version. The result was pure deliciousness.

INGREDIENTS (4 Servings)

- ☐ **1 1/2 lbs. Chicken Breast** (Cut into tenders sized pieces)
- ☐ **6 Cloves Garlic** (Minced)
- ☐ **6 Tbs. Butter** (Divided)
- ☐ **2 oz. Red Onion** (Sliced)
- ☐ **1 Cup Chicken Broth**
- ☐ **1 Cup Heavy Cream**
- ☐ **1/4 Cup Parmesan Cheese** (Grated)
- ☐ **6 oz. Mixed Bell Peppers** (Sliced)
- ☐ **1 tsp. Italian Seasoning**
- ☐ **1/2 tsp. Red Pepper Flakes**
- ☐ **Salt and Pepper** (To Taste)
- ☐ (2 Tbs. Peace and Love)

DIRECTIONS

1. Lightly season the chicken breasts with salt and pepper on both sides.

2. In a large sauté pan, over medium-high heat, pan-sear the chicken tenders in 4 Tbs. butter. Brown on both sides—remove from pan and set aside. (Chicken will not be fully cooking during this stage)

3. Reduce heat to medium, add remaining 2 Tbs. butter and garlic to the pan. Sauté until the butter is browned and the garlic is aromatic—about 2 minutes. Be careful not to burn the garlic as it will taste very bitter.

4. Add sliced red onion and sauté until translucent—about 3-4 minutes.

5. De-glaze the pan with chicken broth. Using a rubber spatula, scrape off and mix in any bits of chicken and garlic. Add Italian seasoning and red pepper flakes. Bring to a boil over medium heat, then reduce heat to low and let simmer 2-3 minutes.

6. Add heavy cream and simmer on low 5-10 minutes to allow sauce to thicken. Mix in Parmesan cheese and salt and pepper to taste.

7. Add peppers to sauce and add chicken back to the pan. Finish cooking chicken in the sauce on low—about 10 minutes.

"JUST LIKE THE REAL THING" LASAGNA

PREP
30min

COOK
40min

PER SERVING

Calories: **486**

Protein: **57 g**

Carbs: **9.5 net g**

Fat: **34 g**

This dish is easy to make and tastes just like the real thing. I served it to my husband without telling him that I made a low carb version and he had no idea. Once I told him, he was even more impressed.

INGREDIENTS (4 Servings)

NOODLES

- [ ] **2 Eggs**
- [ ] **4 oz. Cream Cheese** (Softened)
- [ ] **1/4 Cup Parmesan Cheese** (Grated)
- [ ] **1/4 tsp. Italian Seasoning**
- [ ] **1/4 tsp. Garlic Powder**
- [ ] **1/4 tsp. Onion Powder**
- [ ] **1 1/4 Cup Mozzarella Cheese** (Shredded)

FILLING

- [ ] **1 lb. Ground Beef**
- [ ] **1 Tbs. Dried Onion Flakes**
- [ ] **1 tsp. Dried Oregano**
- [ ] **1 tsp. Garlic Powder**
- [ ] **1 tsp. Dried Basil**
- [ ] **1 1/2 Cups Low Carb Marinara Sauce** (Divided)
- [ ] **3/4 Cup Mozzarella Cheese** (Shredded)
- [ ] **6 Tbs. Whole Milk Ricotta Cheese**
- [ ] **1 tsp. Italian Seasoning**
- [ ] (**2 Tbs. Peace and Love**)

DIRECTIONS

NOODLES

1. This part will take the longest so feel free to make the "noodles" the night before and just leave them in the fridge until you are ready for them.

2. Preheat oven to 375°. Line a 9x13 baking dish with parchment paper.

3. In a large mixing bowl, using a hand mixer, cream together cream cheese and eggs.

4. Next, add Parmesan cheese, Italian seasoning, garlic powder, and onion powder. Mix until all ingredients are well combined. Using a rubber spatula, fold in mozzarella cheese and mix until well incorporated.

5. With a rubber spatula, spread the mixture into the baking dish, forming a nice even layer. Bake on the middle rack for 20-25 minutes.

6. When the "noodles" are done baking, cool in the fridge for about 20 minutes and then cut into thirds. This makes three perfectly sized "noodle" layers for an 8.5 X 4.5 X 2.5 loaf pan.

FILLING

1. In a large skillet, over medium-high heat, combine ground beef, dried onion flakes, oregano, garlic powder, dried basil and a pinch of salt. Cook until meat is browned.

2. Drain excess fat from pan and add 3/4 Cup marinara sauce to meat. Reduce heat to low and simmer for 10 minutes.

3. Pour 1/4 cup marinara sauce into bottom of loaf pan. Top with the first "noodle" layer

4. Layer a third of the ground beef mixture. Top with 1/4 cup mozzarella cheese, 3 Tbs. ricotta cheese, and cover with another "noodle" layer. Repeat these steps.

5. Cover the top "noodle" layer with remaining ground beef and mozzarella cheese. Sprinkle Italian seasoning over top. Bake for 20 minutes.

CHAPTER 5
SIDES & SNACKS

⚜

MEXICAN CAULI RICE

PREP
15min

COOK
50min

PER SERVING

Calories: **122**

Protein: **1.75 g**

Carbs: **6 net g**

Fat: **9.6 g**

To make riced cauliflower, you can give it a few quick pulses in a food processor or you can simply use a cheese grater. I use a cheese grater and it comes out perfect every time. Grate the cauliflower while it is still raw.

INGREDIENTS (6 Servings)

- ☐ **1/4 Cup Olive Oil**
- ☐ **1/2 Cup Onion** (Diced)
- ☐ **2 Tbs. Garlic** (Minced)
- ☐ **3 Cups Cauliflower** (Riced)
- ☐ **2 Tbs. Cumin**
- ☐ **2 tsp. Chili Powder**
- ☐ **1 tsp. Garlic Salt**
- ☐ **2 Cups Chicken Broth**
- ☐ **8 oz. Stewed Tomatoes with Mexican Seasoning**
- ☐ (2 Tbs. Peace and Love)

DIRECTIONS

1. In a large sauté pan over medium-high heat, add olive oil, onion, and garlic. Sauté for 5 minutes.

2. To the pan, add riced cauliflower, cumin, chili powder and garlic salt. Stirring constantly, cook 6-8 minutes.

3. Add chicken broth and stewed tomatoes. Use a rubber spatula to break up the larger chunks of tomato. Reduce heat to low, cover, and allow to simmer 30-40 minutes or until all the liquid has reduced. Stir occasionally.

BROCCOLI BACON AMANDINE

PREP 15min

COOK 15min

PER SERVING

Calories: **166**

Protein: **5.25 g**

Carbs: **4 net g**

Fat: **14 g**

This dish is further proof that bacon makes everything better. It is so simple, but it takes broccoli to a whole new level. Adding the almonds and bacon to the broccoli is also a great way to get picky kids to eat more green vegetables.

INGREDIENTS (4 Servings)

- ☐ **1 Large Head Broccoli** (Cut into florets)
- ☐ **4 Slices Bacon** (Cooked Crisp and Crumbled)
- ☐ **3 Cloves Garlic** (Minced)
- ☐ **1/2 Cup Raw Almonds** (Crushed)
- ☐ **2 Tbs. Olive Oil**
- ☐ **Salt and Pepper** (To Taste)
- ☐ (2 Tbs. Peace and Love)

DIRECTIONS

1. In a large sauce pan over high heat, bring water to a boil. Boil broccoli until it is crisp/tender—about 10 minutes. Drain water.

2. In a large skillet, over medium heat, cook bacon until crisp. Remove from pan and set aside.

3. To the bacon fat add crushed almonds and garlic. Cook until almonds are toasted. Be careful not to burn the garlic as it will taste very bitter. Using a slotted spoon, scoop almonds and garlic out of the bacon fat.

4. In a large mixing bowl, combine broccoli, bacon, almonds, garlic, and salt and pepper. Toss with olive oil until all ingredients are mixed.

LOADED HASSELBACK "POTATOES"

PREP 15min

COOK 60min

PER SERVING

Calories: **495**

Protein: **13 g**

Carbs: **11.25 net g**

Fat: **42 g**

This recipe is believed to have originated in Sweden and is named after the Stockholm Restaurant, Hasselbacken which first began preparing potatoes this way in the 1700s. It seemed like a no-brainer to make a low-carb version of this simple, yet delicious potato dish and then to smother it in cheese and bacon. Two of my favorite things!

INGREDIENTS (4 Servings)

- ☐ **2 Medium Rutabagas**
- ☐ **1 Stick Salted Butter**
- ☐ **2 Tbs. Garlic** (Minced)
- ☐ **5 Slices Bacon** (Cooked Crisp and Crumbled)
- ☐ **1 Cup Sharp Cheddar Cheese** (Shredded)
- ☐ **1/4 Cup Sour Cream**
- ☐ **2 Green Onions** (Chopped)
- ☐ **Salt and Pepper** (To Taste)
- ☐ (2 Tbs. Peace and Love)

DIRECTIONS

1. Preheat oven to 425°.

2. Peel and rinse Rutabagas. Cut slits in the tops about ¼ inch apart and three-quarters of the way down so that the rutabagas are still attached at the bottom. Gently fan out the slices, forcing them open but still keeping them attached.

3. Between each slice, tuck a thin slice of butter. Spread 1 Tbs. minced garlic over top of each rutabaga. Sprinkle with a little salt and pepper.

4. Wrap rutabagas tightly in foil with the foil coming to a close at the top. This will help retain the garlic butter that seeps from the rutabaga.

5. Place foiled-wrapped rutabagas on a baking sheet and bake for 40 minutes. Remove from oven, open foil and pour melted butter back over top of the rutabagas. Bake uncovered for an additional 10 minutes to allow rutabagas to crisp and become golden brown.

6. Top each rutabaga with a mound of cheddar cheese and crumbled bacon. Bake an additional 10 minutes or until cheese is melted.

7. Top with sour cream and green onions before serving.

PUMPKIN SPICE APPLE CHIPS

	PREP 30min	PER SERVING Serving:
x3	COOK 3hours	About 13 Chips Calories: **24** Protein: **0g** Carbs: **5.2 net g** Fat: **0 g**

These apple chips are the perfect fall treat. While I was making them, my house smelled like I had a pumpkin pie in one oven, and an apple pie in the other. Who needs potpourri with a scent this heavenly.

INGREDIENTS (6 Servings)

- ☐ **2 Medium Apples**
- ☐ **2 Tbs. Pumpkin Pie Spice**
- ☐ **2 Tbs. Sweetener**
- ☐ (2 Tbs. Peace and Love)

DIRECTIONS

1. Preheat oven to 200°. Line 2 baking sheets with parchment paper.
2. Using a mandoline or sharp knife, slice apples as thinly as possible.
3. Place apple slices in a single layer across the parchment paper.
4. Combine pumpkin pie spice and sweetener and sprinkle generously over the apple slices. Place trays in oven. Bake for 2.5-3 hours. Swap trays mid-way through baking.

> **TIP:** You can core the apples first, but I just slice the whole apple and then remove the seeds as I go.

CHILI-LIME MIXED NUTS

 PREP
10min

 COOK
15min

PER SERVING

Serving: ¼ **Cup**

Calories: **167**

Protein: **6 g**

Carbs: **4.5 net g**

Fat: **14 g**

For years I bought the cans of seasoned nuts at the grocery store. It had never dawned on me to make my own. But once it did, there was no looking back. This recipe can be done with any of your favorite low carb nuts and seeds.

INGREDIENTS (12 Servings)

- ☐ **1 Cup Raw Almonds,**
- ☐ **1 Cup Raw Peanuts**
- ☐ **1 Cup Raw Cashews**
- ☐ **3 Tbs. Butter** (Melted)
- ☐ **1 Lime** (Juiced)
- ☐ **1 tsp. Chili Powder**
- ☐ **1 tsp. Cumin**
- ☐ **1/2 tsp. Garlic Salt**
- ☐ **1/2 tsp. Onion Powder**
- ☐ (2 Tbs. Peace and Love)

DIRECTIONS

1. Preheat oven to 350°. Line a baking sheet with parchment paper.

2. In a large mixing bowl combine almonds, peanuts, cashews, melted butter, lime juice, chili powder, cumin, garlic salt, and onion powder. Mix until all nuts are evenly coated.

3. Pour nut mixture in a single layer, spread evenly across the parchment paper.

4. Bake for 10-12 minutes. Let cool before serving.

BALSAMIC SHALLOT MUSHROOMS

PREP
5min

COOK
15min

PER SERVING

Calories: **126**

Protein: **5 g**

Carbs: **6 net g**

Fat: **9 g**

This is the perfect side dish to compliment a nice, juicy steak and a glass of red wine. It is simple to prepare yet has a rich, complex flavor that is sure to make your mouth happy.

INGREDIENTS (4 Servings)

- ☐ **3 Tbs. Salted Butter**
- ☐ **1 Large Shallot** (Minced)
- ☐ **1 lb. Cremini Mushrooms** (Quartered)
- ☐ **1/4 Cup Beef Broth**
- ☐ **1/4 Cup Balsamic Vinegar**
- ☐ **2 Tbs. Italian Flat Leaf Parsley** (Chopped)
- ☐ (2 Tbs. Peace and Love)

DIRECTIONS

1. In a large sauté pan over medium heat, add butter and shallot. Sauté until shallots are tender and translucent—about 3-5 minutes.

2. To the pan, add mushrooms, beef stock, balsamic vinegar and parsley. Increase heat to medium-high, bring to a boil, and then reduce heat to low and let simmer for 8-10 minutes.

SHRIMP FRIED CAULI RICE

PREP
15min

COOK
15min

PER SERVING

Calories: **98**

Protein: **5.5 g**

Carbs: **4.8 net g**

Fat: **5.5 g**

To make riced cauliflower, you can give it a few quick pulses in a food processor or use a cheese grater. I use a cheese grater and it comes out perfect every time. Grate the cauliflower while it is still raw. If you do not have a wok, this recipe can be done in a large sauté pan.

INGREDIENTS (6 Servings)

- ☐ **2 Tbs. Butter** (Divided)
- ☐ **2 Tbs. Garlic** (Minced)
- ☐ **2 Green Onions** (Chopped, including the white portion)
- ☐ **1/2 Medium Head Cauliflower** (Riced)
- ☐ **4 Baby Carrots** (Thinly sliced on a bias)
- ☐ **1/2 Cup Frozen Peas**
- ☐ **1/2 Cup Bay Shrimp**
- ☐ **3 Tbs. Soy Sauce**
- ☐ **2 Eggs**
- ☐ (2 Tbs. Peace and Love)

DIRECTIONS

1. In a non-stick wok over medium-high heat, add 1 Tbs. butter, garlic, and the white portion of the onions. Sauté 2 minutes.

2. Add cauliflower, carrots and remaining 1 Tbs. butter and sauté, stirring constantly for 6-7 minutes.

3. Next, stir in the peas, bay shrimp, and soy sauce and sauté, stirring constantly for 3-4 minutes.

4. Push all ingredients to one side of the wok. On the other side, crack the eggs and lightly scramble and then mix them in with the rest of the ingredients. Sauté 2-3 more minutes. Garnish with green onions before serving.

SALT & PEPPER VEGGIE CHIPS

PREP
30min

COOK
30min

PER SERVING

Serving:
About 20 Chips
Calories: **50**
Protein: **1.5 g**
Carbs: **9 net g**
Fat: **1 g**

For frying these chips I use avocado oil because it has a very high smoke point and is my favorite healthy oil. You may need to change the oil out halfway through to avoid the second half of your chips turning out soggy. Fry each vegetable in separate batches as they will all have varying fry times.

INGREDIENTS (6 Servings)

- ☐ **2 Large Carrots**
- ☐ **1 Large Sweet Potato**
- ☐ **3 Beets**
- ☐ **2 Medium Celeriac**
- ☐ **Sea Salt**
- ☐ **Onion Powder**
- ☐ **Black Pepper**
- ☐ (2 Tbs. Peace and Love)

DIRECTIONS

1. Peel and clean vegetables. Using a sharp knife or mandolin, thinly slice vegetables in 1/16 inch slices. Line the slices on paper towels and sprinkle with a little salt. The salt will help draw out excess moisture.

2. Using a deep skillet or wok, heat 2 inches of oil over high heat. Once hot, drop vegetable slices into the oil. Be careful not to put too many in at once. Fry until slightly browned and the edges start to curl. Remove from oil and cool on paper towels.

3. Sprinkle with sea salt, onion powder, and black pepper.

GARLIC PARMESAN BAKED TORTILLA CHIPS

PREP
10min

COOK
20min

PER SERVING

Calories: **287**

Protein: **13 g**

Carbs: **6.5 net g**

Fat: **24 g**

Isn't it great to know that you can still have chips and salsa without blowing your low-carb diet? This is a great little snack and the entire batch is only 13 net grams of carbs. Feel free to indulge in some guilt-free snacking.

INGREDIENTS (2 Servings)

- ☐ **2 Large Low Carb Tortillas**
- ☐ **3 Tbs. Salted Butter** (Melted)
- ☐ **1 Tbs. Garlic Powder**
- ☐ **1 Tbs. Italian Seasoning**
- ☐ **1/4 Cup Parmesan Cheese** (Grated)
- ☐ (2 Tbs. Peace and Love)

DIRECTIONS

1. Preheat oven to 350°.

2. Brush melted butter on one side of tortillas. Mix garlic powder and Italian seasoning together and sprinkle generously over the buttered side of both tortillas.

3. Using a pizza cutter, cut the tortillas into triangles (or strips), whichever you prefer.

4. On a lightly oiled baking sheet, arrange the chips in a single layer, dry side down. Bake for 10 minutes.

5. Remove tray from over, flip the chips over and brush the other side with butter and coat with Parmesan cheese.

6. Bake 10-12 minutes longer.

SPICY BUFFALO ROASTED NUTS

 PREP
10min

COOK
15min

PER SERVING

Serving: ¼ **Cup**

Calories: **200**

Protein: **7 g**

Carbs: **3.5 net g**

Fat: **17 g**

I love buffalo wing sauce. I could put it on just about anything. These spicy nuts are a great snack to make ahead of time and portion out for later. Stash them in your bag, desk, cupboard for when those sneaky cravings appear. This recipe can be done with any of your favorite low carb nuts and seeds.

INGREDIENTS (12 Servings)

- ☐ **1 Cup Raw Almonds,**
- ☐ **1 Cup Raw Pepitas**
- ☐ **1 Cup Raw Cashews**
- ☐ **4 Tbs. Buffalo Wing Sauce**
- ☐ **3 Tbs. Butter** (Melted)
- ☐ **1/2 tsp. Chili Powder**
- ☐ **1/2 tsp. Onion Powder**
- ☐ **1/2 tsp. Garlic Salt**
- ☐ **Pinch Cayenne Pepper**
- ☐ (2 Tbs. Peace and Love)

DIRECTIONS

1. Preheat oven to 350°. Line a baking sheet with parchment paper.

2. In a large mixing bowl combine almonds, pepitas, cashews, melted butter, buffalo wing sauce, chili powder, onion powder, garlic salt and cayenne. Mix until all nuts are evenly coated.

3. Pour nut mixture in a single layer, spread evenly across the parchment paper.

4. Bake for 10-12 minutes. Let cool before serving.

PARMESAN DIJON ROASTED CAULIFLOWER

PREP
10min

COOK
45min

PER SERVING

Calories: **195**

Protein: **6 g**

Carbs: **6 net g**

Fat: **13 g**

I can never get enough of oven-roasted vegetables. The Parmesan and Dijon really add a special element to this dish. I love to pair this side dish with pork chops or blackened chicken.

INGREDIENTS (4 Servings)

- ☐ **1 Large Head Cauliflower** (Trimmed and Cut into florets)
- ☐ **1/4 Cup Dijon Mustard**
- ☐ **1/4 Cup Mayonnaise**
- ☐ **1/4 Cup Parmesan Cheese** (Grated)
- ☐ **1/2 tsp. Garlic Powder**
- ☐ **1/2 tsp. Onion Powder**
- ☐ **1/2 tsp. Dried Thyme**
- ☐ **1/4 tsp. Italian Seasoning**
- ☐ **1/4 tsp. Oregano**
- ☐ **1/4 tsp. Sea Salt**
- ☐ (2 Tbs. Peace and Love)

DIRECTIONS

1. Preheat oven to 400°. Line a baking sheet with parchment paper.

2. In a large mixing bowl, combine Dijon, mayonnaise, Parmesan cheese, garlic powder, onion powder, thyme, Italian seasoning, oregano and sea salt. Mix until all ingredients are well incorporated.

3. Add cauliflower florets to bowl and toss in Dijon mixture until all pieces are evenly coated.

4. Spread cauliflower in a single layer on the parchment paper. Bake on middle rack for 45 minutes.

CARAMELIZED ONION & HORSERADISH CAULIFLOWER MASH

PREP 15min

COOK 45min

PER SERVING

Calories: **120**

Protein: **2.5 g**

Carbs: **4.5 net g**

Fat: **9.5 g**

This is a simple side dish that pair nicely with most meats. I love to serve it with the Blackened Pork Chops with Balsamic Peppers & Onions recipe on page 63.

INGREDIENTS (8 Servings)

- ☐ **1 Large Head Cauliflower** (Cleaned and Trimmed)
- ☐ **1 Medium Onion** (Thinly Slices)
- ☐ **2 Tbs. Garlic** (Minced)
- ☐ **2 Tbs. Butter**
- ☐ **2 Tbs. Olive Oil**
- ☐ **1/4 Cup Sour Cream**
- ☐ **1/4 Cup Horseradish**
- ☐ **Salt and Pepper** (To Taste)
- ☐ (2 Tbs. Peace and Love)

DIRECTIONS

1. In a large sauté pan over low-medium heat, add onion, garlic, butter, olive oil and salt and pepper. Cook until onions are nice and caramelized—about 30 minutes.

2. While the onions are caramelizing, fill a large sauce pan with 1 inch of water. Over high heat, steam the cauliflower, whole and, covered, until fork tender—about 15 minutes.

3. Once the cauliflower is fork tender, drain the water and leave cauliflower in the hot pan to help draw out some of the excess moisture.

4. Fork mash the cauliflower in the pan. Add caramelized onions, sour cream, horseradish sauce, and salt and pepper to the pan. Using a potato masher, mash all ingredients together.

OVEN ROASTED SQUASH MEDLEY

PREP
10min

COOK
30min

PER SERVING

Calories: **123**

Protein: **2 g**

Carbs: **4.5 net g**

Fat: **4 g**

Roasted squash makes an excellent side dish. Not only it is low in carbs, it is also very low in calories. They are also a good source of folate, potassium, vitamin A, and magnesium.

INGREDIENTS (4 Servings)

- ☐ **1 Large Zucchini**
- ☐ **1 Large Mexican Squash**
- ☐ **1 Large Yellow Squash**
- ☐ **1 tsp. Garlic Salt**
- ☐ **1 tsp. Onion Powder**
- ☐ **1 tsp. Oregano**
- ☐ **3 Tbs. Olive Oil**
- ☐ (2 Tbs. Peace and Love)

DIRECTIONS

1. Preheat oven to 400°. Line a baking sheet with parchment paper.

2. Slice the zucchini, Mexican squash, and yellow squash in half lengthwise and then cut into 1/2 inch slices. Arrange the slices in a single layer on the parchment paper.

3. Drizzle with olive oil and sprinkle with garlic salt, onion powder, and oregano.

4. Bake 30 minutes on middle rack.

ALMOND JOY FRUIT & NUT BARS

PREP
15min

COOK
None

PER SERVING

Serving: **1 Bar**

Calories: **162**

Protein: **4 g**

Carbs: **17 net g**

Fat: **9 g**

I can't believe that something with so few ingredients can taste so good. These bars are great for when that evil little sweet tooth hits. They are a much healthier alternative than reaching for a candy bar. I also like to eat them before my workouts.

INGREDIENTS (8 Servings)

- ☐ **1 Cup Almonds**
- ☐ **1 Cup Deglet Noor Dates** (Pitted and Chopped)
- ☐ **1/4 Cup Unsweetened Coconut** (Shredded)
- ☐ **2 Tbs. Unsweetened Cocoa Powder**
- ☐ (2 Tbs. Peace and Love)

DIRECTIONS

1. Grind almonds in food processor until they are finely chopped. Add dates, coconut, and cocoa powder. Pulse until all ingredients are combined and evenly sized.

2. Pour mixture between two sheets of plastic wrap. Use your hands to press and form the mixture into a compact rectangular shape. Wrap the plastic wrap around it and refrigerate for 1 hour. This will allow it to firm up and make it easier to cut into bars.

3. Remove from fridge and cut into 8 bars. I individually wrap the bars in plastic wrap and store them in the fridge.

CHAPTER 6
SAUCES, DIPS, & DRESSINGS

PREP
15min

COOK
None

PER SERVING

Calories: **105**

Protein: **.15 g**

Carbs: **3.5 net g**

Fat: **9 g**

JON'S GUACAMOLE

This is a guest recipe by my handsome husband Jon. I call him the guacamole master. If you love garlic, and you love guacamole, then you will love this recipe. This guac does not have cilantro in it as guacamole traditionally does. He leaves it out because he likes me, and I don't like cilantro.

INGREDIENTS (16 Servings)

- [ ] **6 Large Avocados** (Peeled and Pitted)
- [ ] **4 Tbs. Garlic** (Minced)
- [ ] **1 Lime** (Juiced)
- [ ] **2 tsp. Garlic Salt**
- [ ] **1 tsp. Cayenne Pepper**
- [ ] **1/2 Medium Onion** (Grated)
- [ ] **1 Medium Tomato** (Chopped)
- [ ] **12 Pickled Jalapeno Slices** (Chopped)
- [ ] (2 Tbs. Peace and Love)

DIRECTIONS

1. To a large mixing bowl, mash together avocado, garlic, lime juice, garlic salt and cayenne pepper.

2. Using a microplane grater, grate the onion into the avocado mixture. Mix in tomatoes and jalapenos.

AVOCADO RANCH DRESSING

PREP 10min

COOK None

PER SERVING

Serving: **2 Tbs.**

Calories: **100**

Protein: **.7 g**

Carbs: **1 net g**

Fat: **10 g**

I have had an almost embarrassing love affair with ranch dressing for as long as I can remember. There is almost no limit to what I will put it on. The second I made this recipe, I vowed never to buy store bought ranch again. I have a feeling you just may make the same vow. This ranch is fabulous as a dip or a salad dressing.

INGREDIENTS (12 Servings)

- ☐ **1/2 Large Avocado** (Peeled and Pitted)
- ☐ **1/2 Cup Mayonnaise**
- ☐ **1/2 Cup Sour Cream**
- ☐ **1 Clove Garlic** (Minced)
- ☐ **1 Tbs. Fresh Parsley** (Chopped)
- ☐ **1 Tbs. Fresh Chives** (Chopped)
- ☐ **2 tsp. Apple Cider Vinegar**
- ☐ **1 tsp. Fresh Dill** (Chopped)
- ☐ **1/2 tsp. Onion Powder**
- ☐ **1/4 tsp. Sea Salt**
- ☐ **1/8 tsp. Black Pepper**
- ☐ (2 Tbs. Peace and Love)

DIRECTIONS

1. In a large mixing bowl, fork mash the avocado. To the bowl add the mayonnaise, sour cream, garlic, parsley, chives, apple cider vinegar, dill, onion powder, sea salt, and black pepper. Mix until all ingredients are well incorporated. Refrigerate at least one hour before serving.

ARTICHOKE GARLIC AIOLI

PREP
10min

COOK
None

PER SERVING

Serving: **2 Tbs.**

Calories: **95**

Protein: **.25 g**

Carbs: **1.5 net g**

Fat: **10 g**

This dip is wonderful with seafood and is a great alternative to tartar sauce.

INGREDIENTS (12 Servings)

- ☐ **3/4 Cup Mayonnaise**
- ☐ **3 Whole Artichoke Hearts**
- ☐ **3 Tbs. Garlic** (Minced)
- ☐ **1/2 Fresh Lemon** (Juiced)
- ☐ **1/2 tsp. Onion Powder**
- ☐ **1/2 tsp. Garlic Salt**
- ☐ **1/4 tsp. Black Pepper**
- ☐ **A Few Sprigs Fresh Parsley**
- ☐ (2 Tbs. Peace and Love)

DIRECTIONS

1. Combine mayonnaise, artichoke hearts, garlic, lemon juice, onion powder, garlic salt, black pepper, and parsley in a food processor. Pulse until well blended and creamy. Alternately, this may be done in a blender.

GREEK ONION DIP

 PREP
10min

 COOK
30min

PER SERVING

Serving: **¼ Cup**

Calories: **70**

Protein: **1.5 g**

Carbs: **3 net g**

Fat: **6 g**

One of my fondest food memories of barbecues and family gatherings as a kid was the onion dip and chips. I was that easy to please. It was hard to believe that one pack of dried onion soup and sour cream could make such an incredible taste. This is my adult, healthier, homemade version of that old favorite. Making this recipe with Greek yogurt packs it with extra protein. Serve it alongside a vegetable tray and you have a low carb party appetizer that won't break the carb bank.

INGREDIENTS (16 Servings)

- ☐ **2 Medium Sweet Onions** (Thinly Sliced)
- ☐ **2 Tbs. Butter**
- ☐ **2 Tbs. Olive Oil**
- ☐ **2 Tbs. Cooking Sherry**
- ☐ **2 Tbs. Garlic** (Minced)
- ☐ **16 oz. Plain Greek Yogurt**
- ☐ **1 Tbs. Worcestershire Sauce**
- ☐ **1 1/2 tsp. Garlic Salt**
- ☐ **1 tsp. Onion Powder**
- ☐ **1/2 tsp. Dried Thyme**
- ☐ **1/4 tsp. Black Pepper**
- ☐ **2 Green Onions** (Chopped)
- ☐ (2 Tbs. Peace and Love)

DIRECTIONS

1. In a large sauté pan over low-medium heat, add onions, butter, olive oil, cooking sherry, garlic, and a dash of salt and pepper. Cook until onions are nice and caramelized— about 30 minutes.

2. In a large mixing bowl, combine Greek yogurt, Worcestershire sauce, garlic salt, onion powder, thyme, and pepper.

3. Mix caramelized onions in with Greek yogurt. Garnish with chopped green onions. This dip is best served after refrigerating for several hours to let the flavors come together.

SUN-DRIED TOMATO GARLIC DIP

PREP
10min

COOK
None

PER SERVING

Serving: **2 Tbs.**

Calories: **98**

Protein: **.5 g**

Carbs: **1.5 net g**

Fat: **10 g**

I am at a loss for words to describe this dip. In addition to being a great dip, it would also be great on chicken, as a pasta sauce, a sandwich spread, just by the spoonful, you name it. It is so versatile and delicious.

INGREDIENTS (12 Servings)

- ☐ **3/4 Cup Mayonnaise**
- ☐ **1.5 oz. Sun-Dried Tomatoes**
- ☐ **3 Tbs. Garlic** (Minced)
- ☐ **2 Tbs. Parmesan** (Grated)
- ☐ **1/2 Fresh Lemon** (Juiced)
- ☐ **1/2 tsp. Onion Powder**
- ☐ **1/4 tsp. Garlic Salt**
- ☐ **1/4 tsp. Black Pepper**
- ☐ **A Few Sprigs Fresh Parsley**
- ☐ (2 Tbs. Peace and Love)

DIRECTIONS

1. Combine mayonnaise, sun-dried tomatoes, garlic, Parmesan, lemon juice, onion powder, garlic salt, black pepper, and parsley in a food processor. Pulse until well blended and creamy. Alternately, this may be done in a blender.

BALSAMIC SHALLOT VINAIGRETTE

 PREP
10min

 COOK
None

PER SERVING

Serving: **2 Tbs.**

Calories: **106**

Protein: **0 g**

Carbs: **2 net g**

Fat: **11 g**

There are so many things I love about this recipe. I love that this vinaigrette can have such a complex flavor with such simple ingredients. I also love that it is missing all of the nasty, preservatives and ingredients that I cannot even pronounce that are in most store bought dressings. It also makes a great marinade for chicken.

INGREDIENTS (20 Servings)

- ☐ **1 Cup Balsamic Vinegar**
- ☐ **1 Cup Avocado Oil**
- ☐ **1/2 Fresh Lemon** (Juiced)
- ☐ **1 Small Shallot** (Finely Chopped)
- ☐ **1 Tbs. Red Pepper Flakes**
- ☐ **1 Tbs. Onion Salt**
- ☐ (2 Tbs. Peace and Love)

DIRECTIONS

1. Combine all ingredients and shake until ingredients are well incorporated. As we all know, oil and vinegar do not stay mixed. Shake well before each use. Keep refrigerated. I recommend making it a day ahead of time and allowing it to refrigerate for 24 hours to let the flavors come together.

> **TIP:** If you do not have avocado oil, you can substitute olive oil in this recipe. If you do not have fresh ground onion salt, you can substitute sea salt and dried onion flakes.

BACON RANCH DIP

 PREP
10min

 COOK
None

PER SERVING

Serving: **2 Tbs.**

Calories: **107**

Protein: **2 g**

Carbs:

Less than 1 net g

Fat: **11 g**

This recipe combines two of my all-time favorite things...bacon and ranch dressing. If no one was looking, I might just make a meal solely out of this dip. Okay, not really but I do like it that much. It is great as a dip or as a salad dressing.

INGREDIENTS (12 Servings)

- ☐ **5 Strips Bacon** (Cooked Crisp and Crumbled)
- ☐ **1/2 Cup Mayonnaise**
- ☐ **1/2 Cup Sour Cream**
- ☐ **1 Clove Garlic** (Minced)
- ☐ **1 Tbs. Fresh Parsley** (Chopped)
- ☐ **1 Tbs. Fresh Chives** (Chopped)
- ☐ **2 tsp. Apple Cider Vinegar**
- ☐ **1 tsp. Fresh Dill** (Chopped)
- ☐ **1/2 tsp. Onion Powder**
- ☐ **1/4 tsp. Sea Salt**
- ☐ **1/8 tsp. Black Pepper**
- ☐ (2 Tbs. Peace and Love)

DIRECTIONS

1. In a large mixing bowl, combine bacon, mayonnaise, sour cream, garlic, parsley, chives, apple cider vinegar, dill, onion powder, sea salt, and black pepper. Mix until all ingredients are well incorporated. Refrigerate at least one hour before serving.

SPICY SOUR CREAM CHIVE DIP

PREP
10min

COOK
None

PER SERVING
Serving: **2 Tbs.**
Calories: **46**
Protein: **.7 g**
Carbs:
Less than 1 net g
Fat: **3.5 g**

This would be a great dip to take to a party with a big veggie tray. It packs a lot of flavor and has just the right amount of spiciness.

INGREDIENTS (12 Servings)

- ☐ **1 Cup Sour Cream**
- ☐ **1/4 Cup Horseradish Dijon Mustard**
- ☐ **4 Chives** (Chopped)
- ☐ **1 Tbs. Lemon Juice**
- ☐ **1/4 tsp. Garlic Salt**
- ☐ (2 Tbs. Peace and Love)

DIRECTIONS

1. In a large mixing bowl, combine sour cream, horseradish Dijon mustard, chives, lemon juice and garlic salt. Stir until all ingredients are well incorporated. Refrigerate 1 hour before serving.

CREAMY GARLIC PARMESAN ITALIAN DRESSING

PREP
10min

COOK
None

PER SERVING
Serving: **2 Tbs.**
Calories: **113**
Protein:
Less than 1 g
Carbs:
Less than 1 net g
Fat: **11 g**

Once you start making your own salad dressings, it's hard to stop. The great thing about this dressing is that it is made up of ingredients you probably already have on hand.

INGREDIENTS (21 Servings)

- ☐ **1 Cup Olive Oil**
- ☐ **3/4 Cup Red Wine Vinegar**
- ☐ **2 Cloves Garlic** (Minced)
- ☐ **1 Small Shallot** (Finely Chopped)
- ☐ **1/4 Cup Parmesan Cheese** (Grated)
- ☐ **3 Tbs. Mayonnaise**
- ☐ **2 Tbs. Dijon Mustard**
- ☐ **2 Tbs. Dried Onion Flakes**
- ☐ **1 1/2 tsp. Red Pepper Flakes**
- ☐ **1 1/2 tsp. Garlic Salt**
- ☐ **1 1/2 tsp. Italian Seasoning**
- ☐ **1/2 tsp. Black Pepper**
- ☐ (2 Tbs. Peace and Love)

DIRECTIONS

1. Combine all ingredients and shake until ingredients are well incorporated. Shake well before each use. Keep refrigerated. I recommend making it a day ahead of time and allowing it to refrigerate for 24 hours to let the flavors come together.

ITALIAN VINAIGRETTE DRESSING

PREP
10min

COOK
None

PER SERVING

Serving: **2 Tbs.**

Calories: **103**

Protein: **0 g**

Carbs:

Less than 1 net g

Fat: **11 g**

This vinaigrette makes a great light salad dressing. It would also make a great marinade for poultry or seafood.

INGREDIENTS (19 Servings)

- ☐ **1 Cup Olive Oil**
- ☐ **3/4 Cup Red Wine Vinegar**
- ☐ **1 Clove Garlic** (Minced)
- ☐ **1 Small Shallot** (Finely Chopped)
- ☐ **2 Tbs. Dijon Mustard**
- ☐ **2 Tbs. Dried Onion Flakes**
- ☐ **1 1/2 tsp. Red Pepper Flakes**
- ☐ **1 1/2 tsp. Garlic Salt**
- ☐ **1 1/2 tsp. Italian Seasoning**
- ☐ (2 Tbs. Peace and Love)

DIRECTIONS

1. Combine all ingredients and shake until ingredients are well incorporated. Shake well before each use. Keep refrigerated. I recommend making it a day ahead of time and allowing it to refrigerate for 24 hours to let the flavors come together.

AVOCADO HUMMUS

PREP
10min

COOK
None

PER SERVING

Serving: ¼ **Cup**

Calories: **80**

Protein: **2 g**

Carbs: **2.4 net g**

Fat: **7.2 g**

Hummus has been one of my favorite foods since the first time I tasted it. I could easily take down a whole dish of it singlehandedly. My days of eating garbanzo beans in abundance are long over. Therefore I created this healthier low-carb, paleo version so that when I eat a whole dish of it, I won't feel nearly as guilty. This is a great dip to accompany a vegetable platter. My husband also likes to use it as a dressing on his salads.

INGREDIENTS (10 Servings)

- ☐ **1 Large Zucchini** (Peeled and Cubed)
- ☐ **1 Medium Avocado** (Peeled, Pitted and Cubed)
- ☐ **1/2 Lemon** (Juiced)
- ☐ **1/4 Cup Creamy Roasted Tahini with Sea Salt**
- ☐ **3 Large Cloves Garlic** (Minced)
- ☐ **1 Tbs. Olive Oil**
- ☐ **1 tsp. Cumin**
- ☐ **1 tsp. Sea Salt**
- ☐ (2 Tbs. Peace and Love)

DIRECTIONS

1. In a food processor, combine zucchini, avocado, lemon juice, tahini, garlic, olive oil, cumin and sea salt. Pulse until smooth and creamy.

2. Refrigerate at least one hour prior to serving.

CHAPTER 7

MISCELLANEOUS

CINNAMON CREAM CHEESE FROSTING

PREP
15min

COOK
None

PER SERVING

Calories: **482**

Protein: **5 g**

Carbs: **5 net g**

Fat: **50 g**

This frosting is so simple, yet rich and delicious. I barely got a chance to use it before my family ate it straight out of the bowl. This frosting would be great on cake, cupcakes, and breads.

INGREDIENTS (1 Batch)

- ☐ **4 oz. Cream Cheese** (Softened)
- ☐ **2 Tbs. Butter**
- ☐ **1/2 tsp. Vanilla Extract**
- ☐ **1/2 tsp. Cinnamon**
- ☐ **1/2 Cup Powdered Erythritol**
- ☐ (2 Tbs. Peace and Love)

DIRECTIONS

1. Using a hand mixer or food processor, cream together cream cheese, and butter. Mix in vanilla extract and cinnamon. Gradually fold in powdered erythritol. Mix until all ingredients are well incorporated.

BLACKENED SEASONING

PREP
5min

COOK
None

PER SERVING

Calories: **96**

Protein: **4 g**

Carbs: **12 net g**

Fat: **3 g**

MISCELLANEOUS

This is a nice, spicy seasoning that is great on just about any meat, poultry or seafood. Some of my favorite uses for it are on pork chops, chicken, and salmon.

INGREDIENTS (1 Batch)

- ☐ 1 1/2 Tbs. Paprika
- ☐ 1 Tbs. Garlic Powder
- ☐ 1 Tbs. Onion Powder
- ☐ 1 Tbs. Thyme
- ☐ 1 tsp. Cayenne Pepper
- ☐ 1 tsp. Basil
- ☐ 1 tsp. Cumin
- ☐ 1 tsp. Celery Salt
- ☐ 1/2 tsp. Oregano
- ☐ (2 Tbs. Peace and Love)

DIRECTIONS

1. Combine all spices and store in an air tight container.

TACO SEASONING

PREP
15min

COOK
25min

PER SERVING

Calories: **133**

Protein: **6 g**

Carbs: **17 net g**

Fat: **5 g**

This seasoning is a tad on the spicy side. If you do not care for spicy foods, simply reduce or omit the cayenne pepper. Use 4 Tbs. of seasoning for each pound of meat used. To make taco meat, simply brown the ground beef, ground turkey or meat of choice and drain excess grease. Add 2/3 cup water and 4 Tbs. seasoning, reduce heat to low and let simmer 3-4 minutes until thickened.

INGREDIENTS (1 Batch)

- ☐ **2 Tbs. Chili Powder**
- ☐ **2 Tbs. Cumin**
- ☐ **2 tsp. Onion Powder**
- ☐ **2 tsp. Garlic Powder**
- ☐ **2 tsp. Celery Salt**
- ☐ **1/2 tsp. Cayenne Pepper**
- ☐ **1/2 tsp. Black Pepper**
- ☐ **1/2 tsp. Garlic Salt**
- ☐ (2 Tbs. Peace and Love)

DIRECTIONS

1. Combine all ingredients and store in an air tight container when not in use.

ITALIAN BREADING

PREP
10min

COOK
None

PER SERVING

Calories: **654**

Protein: **65 g**

Carbs: **5 net g**

Fat: **42 g**

This breading is great for making fried mozzarella, chicken parmesan, or any of your favorite fried appetizers. It is very versatile and you would never know that you weren't eating something coated with Italian breadcrumbs.

INGREDIENTS (1 Batch)

- ☐ **1 Cup Pork Rinds** (Crushed)
- ☐ **3/4 Cup Parmesan Cheese** (Grated)
- ☐ **1/2 tsp. Garlic Powder**
- ☐ **1/2 tsp. Onion Powder**
- ☐ **1/2 tsp. Oregano**
- ☐ **1/2 tsp. Italian Seasoning**
- ☐ (2 Tbs. Peace and Love)

DIRECTIONS

1. Combine all ingredients in a food processor and give a couple of quick pulses. Your breading is now ready to use.

PIZZA CRUST

PREP 15min

COOK 25min

PER SERVING

Serving: **1 Slice**

Calories: **167**

Protein: **12 g**

Carbs: **2 net g**

Fat: **12 g**

When cooked perfectly, this crust is an excellent low-carb, gluten free alternative to standard pizza crust. You no longer have to miss pizza on your low carb diet. Here is a little secret... If you make this crust in a 9x13 glass baking dish and cut the finished product into thirds, it makes an excellent noodle substitution for lasagna. My "Just Like The Real Thing" Lasagna recipe is featured on page 65.

INGREDIENTS (6 Servings)

- ☐ **2 Eggs**
- ☐ **4 oz. Cream Cheese** (Softened)
- ☐ **1/4 Cup Parmesan Cheese** (Grated)
- ☐ **1/4 tsp. Italian Seasoning**
- ☐ **1/4 tsp. Garlic Powder**
- ☐ **1/4 tsp. Onion Powder**
- ☐ **1 1/4 Cup Mozzarella Cheese** (Shredded)
- ☐ (2 Tbs. Peace and Love)

DIRECTIONS

1. Preheat oven to 375°. Line a 12 inch pizza pan with parchment paper.

2. In a large mixing bowl, using a hand mixer, cream together cream cheese and eggs.

3. Next, add Parmesan cheese, Italian seasoning, garlic powder, and onion powder. Mix until all ingredients are well combined. Using a rubber spatula, fold in mozzarella cheese and mix until well incorporated.

4. With a rubber spatula, scrape the mixture onto the pizza pan and spread, forming a nice even layer.

5. Bake on the middle rack for 20-25 minutes. If you like a crispier crust, you can cook it longer. Just be sure to keep checking on it so it does not burn.

6. When the crust is done baking, let it cool on a cooling rack while still on the parchment paper but not on the pizza pan. After the crust has cooled, slide a spatula under the crust to loosen it from the parchment paper and put it back on the pizza pan. You are now ready to pile on your topping and make your pizza.

DRY ONION SOUP MIX

PREP
5min

COOK
None

PER SERVING

Calories: **110**

Protein: **2 g**

Carbs: **23 net g**

Fat: **0 g**

You will never need packaged onion soup mix again. 4 Tbs. of this mix is equal to one store bought package. This mix really adds something special when mixed with ground beef for burgers on the grill. It also makes a great dip when mixed with sour cream or plain Greek yogurt.

INGREDIENTS (1 Batch)

- ☐ **4 Tbs. Dried Onion Flakes**
- ☐ **2 Tbs. Powdered Beef Bouillon**
- ☐ **1 tsp. Onion Powder**
- ☐ **1 tsp. Garlic Powder**
- ☐ **1 tsp. Dried Parsley**
- ☐ **1/4 tsp. Celery Salt**
- ☐ **1/4 tsp. Black Pepper**
- ☐ (2 Tbs. Peace and Love)

DIRECTIONS

1. Combine all ingredients and store in an air tight container when not in use.

·

INDEX

Lightning Source UK Ltd.
Milton Keynes UK
UKOW02f2119280715

255993UK00001B/199/P

9 780989 122801